Noam Chomsky

Titles in the series Critical Lives present the work of leading cultural figures of the modern period. Each book explores the life of the artist, writer, philosopher or architect in question and relates it to their major works.

Noam Chomsky

Wolfgang B. Sperlich

REAKTION BOOKS

For my family to the left, Susan, Samantha and d'Arcy

Published by Reaktion Books Ltd
33 Great Sutton Street
London EC1V 0DX, UK

www.reaktionbooks.co.uk

First published 2006

Printed and bound in Great Britain
by CPI/Bath Press Ltd, Bath

British Library Cataloguing in Publication Data
Sperlich, Wolfgang B., 1948–
    Noam Chomsky. – (Critical lives)
    1. Chomsky, Noam 2. Linguists – United States – Biography
    I.Title
    410.9'2

ISBN 1 86189 269 1

Contents

Chomsky at work.

1

A Working Life

Not a few of mankind's original thinkers have been colourful figures, led flamboyant lives and thus provided valuable material for many a biography filled with a salacious story or two. Take Friedrich Schiller, the German dramatic rebel and accidental academic. When giving his inaugural lecture at the University of Jena in 1789, he saw that far more people had turned up than could be accommodated in the lecture hall. Rather than let his employers find something bigger nearby, the youthful Schiller seized the moment and marched with the crowd through the streets of Jena to the town hall. There he lectured to an enthusiastic crowd of thousands shouting 'freedom', subsequently enjoying the attention he received from the liberated ladies of the town. Other fighters for freedom and reason, such as Jean-Paul Sartre and Bertrand Russell, led eccentric lives that had the local establishments in uproar. Even a working-class hero like George Orwell could never quite divorce himself from his upper-class public school upbringing, or so his biographers tell us. All such activists – known and unknown – fought their battles to improve the lot of ordinary men and women, and quite a few advanced science and the arts along the way.

Noam Chomsky is one of the most notable contemporary champions of the people. He is also a scientist of the highest calibre. But is he great material for a biography? Certainly not, if you ask the subject. An intensely private man, he is horrified to be considered the main character in any story. He jokes about the notion

Chomsky at work in private.

that people come to see him, listen to him, even adore him, when in fact he is the most boring speaker ever to hit the stage. He gets serious very quickly and tells his audiences that they have come to hear about the 'issues' of our time, issues that are important to them and, as it happens, to him. What is it that he knows and the people don't? Wrong question, he would say. The people merely want to know the truth and they know it is hidden from them by a vast propaganda machine. His skill is to lift the veil and reveal the truth. Anyone can do it, says Chomsky, it only takes some dedicated research and logical reasoning.

Two large problems of the world are known as Plato's problem and Orwell's problem, respectively. Chomsky describes them thus:

> Plato's problem . . . is to explain how we can know so much, given that the evidence available to us is so sparse. Orwell's problem is to explain why we know and understand so little, even though the evidence available to us is so rich.[1]

Orwell's problem is an apt description for any political activist, conveying despair at the lack of action in the face of overwhelming information that would dictate otherwise. Why are we unable to stop wars and genocide? Why are we unable to alleviate poverty? Why are we unable to establish a social order where justice and *égalité* are the norm rather than the exception? Plato's problem on the other hand must appeal to all true scientists, like Chomsky. He would ask, as have Galileo, Descartes and Humboldt before him, 'how do we acquire what we call language based on so little input from our language environment?' How do we know all the rules of language when nobody ever taught us? How can we say things we never said before and never heard before? It cannot be learned behaviour, as perhaps the advertising industry would like to have us believe as it tries to manipulate the people.

Stop there, Chomsky would say, don't mix science with political activism. There is no necessary connection between the two, especially not in his case. Like Einstein's theory of relativity, or Russell's principles of mathematical logic, Chomskyan linguistics takes years of training and dedication to the scientific method to advance new theories and make new discoveries. Political activism on the other hand is the people's domain, and while scientists are people, too, there is no logical rule that says that a good scientist is also a good political activist – and quite obviously less so the other way round – however much we would like to believe in its possibility.

So let's look at Noam Chomsky as two people: the scientist (the linguist) and the political activist. His private life is remarkable for its lack of an extraordinary story line. Given the status he has achieved – quite unintended, as we shall see – and the income and financial security that come with it, Chomsky is the first to point out that he leads a privileged life, at least in comparison to the working classes in America, and more so when set against the abject poverty of the masses of people living in the so-called Third World. What is important about Chomsky, however, is that he is one of those who says what the reasons are for this world of oppression and blatant social injustice. In return he is vilified by the corporate world of power, including the mainstream press, in both the US and Europe – the German news magazine *Der Spiegel* has described Chomsky as 'Ayatollah des antiamerikanischen Hasses' ('the Ayatollah of anti-American hatred').[2]

In 2005 Chomsky celebrated his 77th birthday. He is edging closer to becoming an octogenarian linguist and political activist, and bound to remember the public birthday wishes he received from his wife Carol when he turned 70: 'Well, seventy is nice, but what I'm really looking forward to is eighty!'[3] On his birthday, as on every other day of the year, he receives some 200 e-mails dealing with linguistics, politics and other matters. He answers them all, every day of the week (though, befitting his many responsibilities, a couple of personal assistants help him in the process). In addition he prepares speeches, lecture notes, learned articles, his latest book and other writing tasks. As a retired Emeritus Institute Professor of Linguistics at the Massachusetts Institute of Technology (MIT) he still contributes to teaching and research well beyond the call of duty. Chomsky is a ferocious reader and reads with great attention to detail. Over the years he has acquired an encyclopaedic knowledge. As such he never stops working. His output and achievements are enormous, yet he would say that a humble factory worker on the assembly line produces far more than he has ever done. He is deeply aware that his status within the working classes is a privileged one. Still, the true nature of an academic worker is embodied in Chomsky.

Where does Chomsky's capacity for highly productive and original work come from? One source may well be his genetic endowment: it's 'in his bones', as Chomsky is fond of saying. This is a compliment to his parents, who migrated from the Ukraine and Belarus to the United States in 1913 and, as many a successful immigrant tale goes, established themselves through sheer hard work. Both came from

Dr William and Elsie Chomsky with children David and Noam.

an ultra-orthodox Jewish background. His mother, Elsie, was a teacher and activist who managed the Chomsky family in a fairly traditional way within the narrow constraints of contemporary American dominant culture. His father, William, was also a teacher and distinguished himself as a Hebrew scholar, specializing in Hebrew grammar. Elsie's extended family in New York harboured some highly politicized members, but otherwise his parents were both Roosevelt Democrats, immersed in Deweyite educational theories. Being Jewish meant Hebrew-Zionism, which for them meant something like Ahad Ha'am's cultural Zionism, with Palestine seen as a cultural centre but with the notion of a Jewish state only hovering in the background. Chomsky and his younger brother David, both born in Philadelphia, were certainly brought up in an environment of great mental stimulation, with a focus on educational and social issues based on the Democrat tradition of the US. That their father subjected language to intense investigation was an additional bonus for Noam in particular. The social issues faced in the 1930s were among the most intense in recent history. Quite apart from the social upheavals caused by the Great Depression in the city of their upbringing, there were the great national and international movements to consider. As chronicled in Orwellian literature, the dark shadows of totalitarianism enveloped the whole world. In Philadelphia the shadow of oppression was very real for young Chomsky, even in the streets, since theirs was an anti-Semitic neighbourhood, right-wing Catholic in tone and partly Irish and German in origin.

While his family struggled to maintain FDR-style liberalism, Noam was increasingly influenced by an uncle from New York who told him that there was more to it, much more, including solidarity with the working classes and those increasingly misled and oppressed by domestic and international propaganda. This led him to listen carefully to the different voices and languages around him. While the social circle of the Chomsky family was quite small, there was at least his uncle from New York, who provided rich pickings.

Noam's formal education started remarkably early: barely aged two, he was enrolled in Oak Lane County Day School, a Deweyite experimental school run by Temple University, and stayed there until aged twelve.

Chomsky had a natural predilection for mental work. Critical reading of a vast amount of modern Jewish and socialist-orientated literature, as well as some highly technical works on Hebrew language matters (including his father's doctoral dissertation on David Kimche), honed his mind to a degree that was extraordinary for a twelve-year-old boy. While such progress was quite ordinary in the sense of a natural environment providing all the stimuli, there is also the sense that Chomsky became quite competitive in his quest: a family friend is quoted as saying that he was already trying to 'outdo his parents'.[4] Naturally one would expect that Chomsky's parents would have been delighted to see his early determination for the common cause to make the world a better place. There is no suggestion that he was pushed as a *Wunderkind* or child prodigy, an idea that would have been contrary to the educational ideals his parents practised.

Their Jewish community circles also gave rise to the specific preoccupation with the politics of Zionism. Given the impact on subsequent world history, therein lies one of the great contradictions into which Chomsky became enmeshed from early in his life. The permutation from Zionist to anti-Zionist, as perceived by some, remains one of the most bitter political and cultural arguments of our time, even if the hard evidence has always been on Chomsky's side. That he would discuss such matters with some kids from school, at an age when other kids from the non-Jewish neighbourhood were reading, if anything at all, Superman comics, was not so much surprising as it was unusual in the overall context of American life at the time – or of any time. Even so Chomsky has pointed out that such serious discussions were not the order of things, and that normal kids' play predominated.

Aged ten he contributed an editorial article to his school newspaper concerning the spread of fascism. He still remembers the first sentence as something like 'Austria falls, Czechoslovakia falls, and now Barcelona falls'. Two years later he became immersed in the Spanish anarchist revolution, mainly by hanging out in New York second-hand bookstores (many run by recent anti-fascist refugees) and in the office of the anarchist journal *Freie Arbeiter Stimme*, and by discussions with his uncle. That a ten- to twelve-year-old should grapple with such issues might again seem extraordinary. Chomsky maintains today that even a ten-year-old can understand such issues because they are fundamental and based on common sense, hence accessible to anyone at any age of reason. But it comes as no surprise that Chomsky, in his professional life, has not seen any advances in education of the sort he himself was lucky enough to experience, and that he continues to call for the radical reform of mainstream education in America and elsewhere. The obstacles at hand are those of a society based on authoritarian hierarchical institutions not tolerating such alternative school systems for very long. One of the key lessons learned is that a real and positive education can be obtained, much as the anarcho-syndicalist movements achieved a brief but real workers' society in Barcelona. When Chomsky is described as an anarcho-syndicalist and/or a socialist libertarian, even the more well-meaning detractors refer to his high-minded and utopian idealism, when in fact his common-sense stance, as practised by many before him, has always been a realistic option.

At the age of twelve Chomsky received a surprise when he entered Central High, also in Philadelphia. A good school, it never-theless practised a kind of indoctrination, 'providing a system of false beliefs'.[5] He managed to get excellent grades, but he was per-turbed to realize that, unlike at his first school where excellence was solely measured against oneself, he was expected to do so at the expense of those who got lesser marks. A story from high school life describes his break with a practice that is a common obsession in schools and beyond: competitive sports. Initially cheering for the school football team with everyone else, one day he realized the folly of it, especially as he actually 'hates' his high school. This echoes the endless progression of students who come to hate schools and anything they stand for. Orwell, an author Chomsky admires (with reservations), is famous for denouncing his education in no uncertain terms, and so are countless other literary figures who have the means to make it known.

Escaping the narrow confines of Philadelphia, Chomsky, aged thirteen, began to make regular trips to New York, where he visited his mother's family, a family contained within Jewish working-class culture. As noted before, his uncle, Milton Krauss (married to Chomsky's mother's sister), had a news-stand on Seventy-Second Street that was a magnet for mostly middle-class and professional intellectuals, many of them German émigrés and such. Krauss, a remarkable autodidact, was deeply immersed in psychoanalytic literature at the time, and some of those who gravitated to the news-stand in the evenings were professional psychiatrists and psychoanalysts, again mostly German refugees. (His uncle ended up becoming a very successful lay analyst with a Riverside Drive apartment.) Chomsky thus made friends with an assortment of down-at-heel intellectuals. He recalls this as 'the most influential intellectual culture during my early teens'.[6] Moving freely between the realms of unorthodox Marxism and anarchism, he visited the offices of the *Freie Arbeiter Stimme*. A notable contributor was Rudolf Rocker, who wrote convincingly on the merits of anarchism and political revolution.

One thing that must have impressed the teenage Chomsky was that there were armies of good and well-meaning writers and activists who made absolutely no money out of their endeavours, working hard only to advance the common good, with no material benefit for themselves. This was starkly opposed to the crass capitalism he saw around him in New York and closer to home in Philadelphia, where middle- and upper-class people only worked to advance their own interests and material benefits. The idea of working for others and not for oneself became a matter of principle for young Chomsky. It was the natural state of being in the milieu in which he was now immersed. The Hebrew-Zionist culture of his parents' circles was also very dedicated, not to their own material interests, but rather to the 'cause' of revival of Hebrew culture and language, the Zionist settlement in Palestine, and so on. What Chomsky also learnt at a remarkably early age is that 'bad' people can usurp 'good' ideas, hence ideologies can become meaningless when they are hijacked by people with totalitarian tendencies. Chomsky's absolute disdain of Stalinist commissars is thus equal to that of 'imperialist stooges' like Reagan and Bush in the latter days of American power politics.

Reading, as he was, the works of political pamphleteers and underground writers, he was equally struck by what, in stark comparison, the mainstream press and bookstores had to offer. The contrast could not have been greater. Why? The latter is the product of a huge propaganda machine, a notion Chomsky would later set out to prove in detail. The general paranoia of the war years further intensified the gap between truth and propaganda.

When Chomsky graduated from high school, aged sixteen, he had already completed an upbringing that was shaped by what one might call a fortunate combination of genetic endowment and excellent learning experiences. And yet Chomsky is diffident in ascribing his evolution to these factors alone. Asked in an interview about parental influence he said that 'it's a combination of influence and resistance, which is difficult to sort out. Undoubtedly, the background shaped the kinds of interests and tendencies and directions that I pursued. But it was independent.'[7]

Thus Chomsky from an early age placed much importance on the internal dimension of the mind.

At the time that the Second World War was coming to an end, Chomsky enrolled at the University of Pennsylvania, although he continued to live at home. Doing a general course in philosophy, logic and languages, he was one of those students who take papers because they sound interesting, not because they have anything to do with a chosen professional career. Such idealism was often disappointed by the academic reality, which was a crude continuation of a regimented high school system. Only a few lecturers stood out, like his Arabic language teacher, 'an antifascist exile from Italy who was a marvellous person as well as an outstanding scholar'.[8] Such criteria for academics are hard to come by and Chomsky, like so many before and after him,

Noam Chomsky's
High School
graduation day.

considered dropping out, perhaps to go to Palestine and work in a
kibbutz.

With Chomsky's intensely Jewish background such a move
might have been considered quite the thing to do. Indeed the kibbutzim attracted, then as today, many people from all around the
world, not necessarily because they were Jewish, but because the
kibbutzim system was admired for its cooperative and egalitarian
ways of doing things. At the time there were still some kibbutzim
that advocated Arab-Jewish cooperation and were opposed to the
creation of the Zionist state. It was such a kibbutz that Chomsky
would have liked to work in. One problem, however, was that the
organizations representing kibbutzim in the US were split between

Stalinist and Trotskyite (in Palestine, they were almost all Stalinist), and by his early teens he was a pretty committed anti-Leninist (and, of course, anti-Stalin and anti-Trotsky). These were major issues in those days. While Chomsky has since visited Israel many times, he has remained opposed to a Jewish state. As a pragmatist, however, he does not accept the *fait accompli*.

Two events prevented him going to Palestine for good. One was his childhood friend Carol Schatz: they fell in love. The second was meeting Zellig Harris, a professor of linguistics at the University of Pennsylvania. Harris had established the first department of linguistics anywhere in the United States and can fairly be described as the founder of structural linguistics and discourse analysis in America. He had developed a rigorous set of methods by which all languages can be studied and described. He did this by applying methods of segmentation and classification, and some reconstruction, to find the elements of language. Chomsky was interested.

Better still, Harris's politics were close enough to that of Chomsky. Harris was a critical thinker attracted to the Frankfurt School and psychoanalysis. He leaned to the anti-Bolshevik left – Rosenberg, Pannekoek, Paul Mattick (who was his personal friend and whom Chomsky later came to know as well). However his main engagement was with left anti-state Zionism: the League for Arab-Jewish Rapprochement (bi-national) and, primarily, Avukah, the American left anti-state Zionist organization, of which he was the leading figure. Avukah had enormous influence on many young people in those days – lots of young Jewish radical intellectuals involved in Zionism, but anti-state, anti-Stalinist and anti-Leninist as well. For Chomsky this fitted pretty well with his earlier anarchist involvements, which were Rocker-style anarcho-syndicalism and Pannekoek-style left Marxism.

Harris's teaching methods were unorthodox and he engaged with students on a personal level, eschewing the lecture theatres for the pub or his apartment. Chomsky remembers that 'there used to be a Horn & Hardart's right past 34th Street on Woodland Avenue, and

Carol and Noam Chomsky, 1949.

we'd often meet in the upstairs, or in his apartment in Princeton. His partner was a mathematician; she was working with Einstein.'[9]

Given such stellar constellations – being in love and having found a vocation – Chomsky set to work. By 1949, aged only 21, he was married to Carol (aged 19) and he had completed his BA honours' thesis. From then on his life ran in three major strands: personal, professional, and political activism. To the chagrin of commentators and biographers, Chomsky maintains that these strands are independent of each other. Here we take his word and continue along these lines. Separate chapters deal with his professional life as a linguist and as a political activist.

Since Chomsky married when both he and Carol were students, there was no great plan mapped out for a secure future. Indeed, it looked anything but secure. They put off having children for seven years for this reason, but also because they became immersed in their work. Carol was later to become a linguist in her own right, working as a phonetician, mainly in Romance and acoustic phonetics.

At Cape Cod, Massachusetts, *c.* 1959. From left to right: William Chomsky, Elsie Chomsky, Noam Chomsky, Milton Krauss and Sophie Krauss (Elsie's sister).

She did a few years of graduate work in these areas at Harvard, then dropped out about 1953 and didn't go back until 1967 – when there was a serious possibility that Chomsky might be facing a prison sentence, and they had three children to worry about.

When, in 1951, Chomsky gained a prestigious three-year Fellowship at Harvard, Boston was to be their first major residential move and, as it turned out, their last. They took up a small apartment on Commonwealth Avenue in Allston, a district just south of the Charles River (in 1965 they moved to the Lexington area, where they still live). Carol was able to transfer from the University of Pennsylvania to Radcliffe College, which was then the women's college of Harvard (at the time Harvard was a male-only domain).

One of the great benefits of a Harvard Fellowship was a travel grant designed for young Fellows to see the world. In 1953 the Chomskys set off on their first overseas trip. The main aim was to experience life on a kibbutz in Israel, but various parts of Europe were on the itinerary as well. To travel to Europe in 1953, from the

US, must have been a strange experience. The Second World War had left the US prosperous while in Europe, especially in Germany, war damage was still everywhere. The Marshall Plan had already made an economic impact, but many European cities were still bombed out and a succession of severe winters had left its toll on the working-class populations. The Chomskys travelled from England to France, and then through to Switzerland to Italy (Chomsky would in future make Italy his number one destination, both academically and personally). From there they moved to Israel, a landmark destination as far as their Jewish and Zionist (anti-state) background was concerned. While critical of the direction the state of Israel was taking, they enjoyed their stay at a left-leaning kibbutz, doing mainly hard labour. Zellig and Bruria Harris had picked the kibbutz. They themselves lived there frequently: Bruria ended up living there and in the neighbouring kibbutz all year round, while Zellig stayed for about half the year. The kibbutz belonged to Hashomer Hatzair, the further left of the two main kibbutz movements, and the centre of the kibbutz movement that shared activities with the Arab population – a residue of the old bi-nationalism. There were some misgivings, however, as Chomsky

Carol Chomsky in Israel in 1955.

The Chomsky family, from right to left: Noam, Carol, Aviva, Diane and Harry.

notes, in that he became uneasy with 'the exclusiveness and racist institutional setting'.[10] He was also worried by the blind Stalinism practised there. Still, the impact was such that they seriously thought of returning for good when they were back in Boston.

Two years later they decided that Carol should again go to Israel to check out the feasibility of living there permanently. So in 1955 she went back (Chomsky had just started his teaching position at MIT) but, while she again loved her time in the kibbutz, there appeared to be logistical problems, since Noam would have to work at a university during the week and return to the kibbutz on the weekends. This was not their idea of family life. Carol returned to Boston, where three children were born: Aviva (*b.* 1957), Diane (*b.* 1960) and Harry (*b.* 1967). Aviva was eventually to became an academic, specializing in Central American history and politics; Diane works for a development agency with her Nicaraguan *compañero* in Managua; Harry is a software engineer in California.

The financial worries that might result from Chomsky's political activism (jail or worse) were allayed to a certain degree by Carol, who went back to graduate school and gained a PhD in Linguistics, specializing in child language acquisition; in 1969 she published her first book on the subject.[11] She later secured a teaching position at the Harvard School of Education, working there until 1996. But when

Chomsky was arrested for the first time (in October 1967, meeting Norman Mailer in the cells), and as more serious problems developed a year later, in connection with his work as one of the founders of RESIST, opposed to the Vietnam war, there was alarm that things could get out of hand. Thanks to the incompetence of the FBI, Chomsky was set free, while the authorities pursued the Boston Five (Benjamin Spock, Coffin, Raskin, Ferber and Goodman). While the subsequent trial of Dr Spock and the others was a farce in the eyes of the liberals, there were genuine fears within the extended Chomsky family that reactionary forces might stop at nothing. Carol then took to the streets herself, marching at anti-war rallies with the children in tow. She took the two girls to a women–children silent march in peaceful, dovish Concord, Massachusetts, where they were pelted with tin cans and tomatoes.

Chomsky threw himself into his work with increased vigour: by 1982 he was credited with more than 150 publications. He was now sought after as a guest speaker and lecturer, nationally and internationally. He started to collect honorary degrees and international prizes, entering a period of extensive travel. Schedules became ever tighter. As his public image increased it became a fine art to keep the family private. (It was only once Carol had retired in 1996 – and the children had grown up – that she become a regular travel companion and, indeed, Chomsky's travel manager.)

In the 1970s and '80s, the focus was on Noam's working life. Remembering that he had been made tenured professor at MIT at the age of 33, in 1961, and appointed to the prestigious position of Institute Professor by 1976, he was at the height of his professional career as far as ordinary academics are concerned. Indeed he was very much on his way to becoming an extraordinary academic, having been awarded various honorary degrees from institutions as far as apart as the Universities of London (1967) and Delhi (1972, when he was Nehru lecturer); by 2005 he had accumulated a staggering total of about thirty honorary degrees, awards and prizes.

Chomsky receiving an honorary degree from the University of Florence, 2004.

In demand as a guest lecturer and professor in residence, his travel schedule became an international event. His publications output was at a level that few other academics in their field could match. Despite these successes, however, the academic and political activist Chomsky remained on the outer margin of acceptability. Like a latter-day Bertrand Russell, he was able to mobilize many a popular movement and thus acquire a large number of followers, while the establishment (academic and political) did its best to keep him at arm's length, if not to ostracize him completely, for example putting him on Nixon's infamous hit-list of enemies of the state.

Chomsky's ideas are increasingly traded by way of audio and video-tapes and reach audiences far beyond the established distribution networks. One event that remained largely within the realm of the underground and popular movements was his 1970 visit to Hanoi. While everyone knows about Jane Fonda's visit (and her subsequent apology to the American people for her so-called 'treason'), few are familiar with Chomsky's visit. He had been invited to lecture at the

Polytechnique University in Hanoi, or what was left of it, during a bombing halt when people could come in from the countryside. Many of them hadn't seen a book or article for years, and were desperate to catch up with what was going on in the world. Chomsky lectured for many hours on any topic he knew anything about. He also toured Laos on the way. None of his travels since has been quite so controversial, but in undertaking his visit to Turkey in 2002, he put himself at considerable risk by attending the trial of a Turkish publisher accused of treason for publishing one of Chomsky's books. The defence had asked Chomsky to insist on being a co-defendant, and he agreed. The Security Courts, which were sham justice, dropped the prosecution on the first day, presumably because of the international publicity (mostly in Europe, not much in the us). While in Turkey Chomsky also visited some of the Kurdish areas and spoke up for the Kurds' human rights.

Any summary of the very private life of the Chomskys must inevitably note the many contradictions that arise from the clashes between the private and public spheres of their lives. To date it appears that they have handled it very well and been able to maintain the separation between the private and the public, notwithstanding the current effort to shed light on the former. As pointed out at the beginning of this chapter, the best we can learn from Chomsky's private life is that it is based on a supreme belief in a humanistic education, as passed on from parents to children, as continued in a few good schools and universities, and above all on autodidactism.

2

Linguist and Philosopher

Linguistics, or the study of language, is by some considered an odd science. The essential tool for the study of language is language itself. It is a paradox. However, this has not deterred mankind from investigating and speculating since time immemorial. Indeed it is probably one of the oldest sciences known to mankind and, as Chomsky maintains, it is a science like any other. Doing linguistics is, as Chomsky puts it with good humour, doing what any other natural scientist does: looking for the key under the lamppost, like a drunk, because that's where the light is.[1]

One of the earliest known grammarians and searchers for a key was an Indian linguist named Panini, who, in the fifth century BC devised the rules for Sanskrit morphology. In ancient Greece the study of language became closely associated with philosophy: the paradox of 'all Cretans are liars' reverberates to this day. When classical Greek and Latin became the languages of scholarship throughout much of Europe, there came with it an intense preoccupation with the grammars of these two languages. The 'grammar schools' in the English education system survive to this day, albeit in much reduced form. Not surprisingly, practically all the terminology to do with grammar comes from study of the classics. Greek and Latin grammars were the baseline for all other languages. Grammars of English, French, German, Hebrew, Russian, Arabic, Chinese and of other literate languages became incorporated in a more general study of language then called philology. The history of these languages became of great interest and historical changes were investigated, such as the Great Vowel Shift in Germanic languages. The French Port-Royal grammarians of the seventeenth century instigated another aspect: that of the connection between language and thought. Following in part the French philosopher Descartes, they proposed that grammatical categories and structures were analogous to logical patterns of thought, hence mental constructs. Chomsky was to incorporate these ideas into his Cartesian Linguistics.[2]

In the meantime, though, the philologist tradition with the emphasis on the history of languages gave way to the synchronic study of languages. While the nineteenth century was still mainly concerned with historical linguistics, the twentieth century began to focus on living languages as they were spoken. This meant all languages of the world, the majority of which had no literate traditions. The investigation of speech also meant a refocusing on phonetics and phonology, the study of the sound systems of a language. The theory of a 'phoneme' as the psychological representation of an actual speech sound (phonetic form) became widely accepted.[3] It means that a speaker recognizes a variety of closely related speech sounds as one significant sound that imparts meaning when forming a word.

The English words 'mat' and 'mad', for example, are distinguished only by the phonemes of /t/ and /d/ (it is a convention to place phonemes between slashes). However, the native English-language speaker/listener can accommodate quite a number of different phonetic realizations of the /t/, such as the plain [t] and the aspirated [t^h] (it is a convention to put phonetic sounds between square brackets). In Hindi, however, these two sounds are phonemes, /t/ and /t^h/, which impart different meaning in a word that has otherwise the exact same sounds. As such, different languages have different sets of phonemes, which allow for various phonetic realizations. The set of actual phonetic realizations in all languages of the world is captured in the set known as the International Phonetic Alphabet (IPA). Note that in American English the word 'math' as distinguished from 'mat' determines that there are two phonemes, namely the /t/ and the /th/. The German language, for example, has neither the phoneme /th/ nor any sound that in English is realized as /th/.

This idea that speakers have acquired a narrow set of phonemes from the much wider set of all possible speech sounds is in itself revolutionary, for it points to the further theory that an actual language might be just the narrow realization of a much wider (or deeper) system that applies to all languages – an idea also seized on by Chomsky, minus the proviso, however, that any such underlying systems should have a 'psychological reality'. His position has always been that linguists are seeking real systems, systems that should have reality, just like other parts of biology. Since the domain can be regarded as part of psychology, that means they should have psychological reality, which is just reality in the domain of psychology. There is a huge literature claiming that something 'more' is needed to establish psychological reality, like information about processing. That is just mysticism, in Chomsky's view. Of course, one wants theories of language (or chemistry, etc.) to be verified wherever they can be tested, but nothing more than that is involved. Information about, say, processing does not give some mystical insight into 'reality' that evidence from other psychological experiments fails to give (and informant work, with oneself or another native speaker, is just a kind of psychological experiment, which could be made as precise as one likes, if there is any need).

The birth of modern theoretical linguistics is generally attributed to the Swiss linguist Ferdinand de Saussure (1857–1913), who set the scene by distinguishing between *langue* and *parole*.[4] The former refers to the internal system and structure of language *per se*, while the latter refers to the use of language. Again this is quite a revolutionary concept inasmuch as previously it was commonly thought that language use (as communication) determines the structure of language. Indeed, the idea is still alive and well today and serves as an antidote to Chomskyan linguistics. Saussure made, as did Chomsky later on, the principled distinction on the grounds that all people seem to have the same language capacity, but that different people seem to make use of this language capacity in vastly different ways. According to this theory, the language capacity comes first and language use second. The latter has only a minor influence on the former. One should note though that there is a difference in how Saussure and Chomsky conceive of *langue*: for Saussure *langue* was a social concept (it is societies that have a *langue*), while for Chomsky the corresponding concept is one of individual psychology.

Saussure also introduced the semantic dichotomy of the *signifiant* and the *signifé*. For example the English word 'cat' (as a *signifiant*) refers to a certain feline animal (the *signifé*) we know so well. There seems to be only an arbitrary connection between the form of the word (the sound or the written form) and what it stands for. A language unrelated to English may have a totally different sounding word for 'cat'. While Chomsky always thought of this problem as uninteresting (or even trivial), it was the French philosophers of the modern era who made much of it. Indeed Chomsky points to Aristotle, who long ago made the observation that language involves sound–meaning connections, which are, of course, arbitrary.

Early twentieth-century linguistics, however, still proceeded along the lines of the Prague School, which focused on phonology. Roman Jakobson (1898–1983), one of the founders of that school,[5] was to become a friend of Chomsky, having first met him at Harvard University in 1951. Linguistics as the new kid on the science block took another twist in the meantime. On the one hand linguistics entered the domain of logical positivism via Bertrand Russell, who devised the principles of mathematics on the logic of language (or the language of logic), while on the other American linguistics had became heavily influenced by anthropology via Franz Boas (1858–1942), Edward Sapir (1884–1939) and Benjamin Whorf (1897–1941), to name the key players of the time. The Sapir-Whorf hypothesis that different languages generate different world views reverberates to this day. A kind of reverse history was repeated later when the French anthropologist Claude Lévi-Strauss (*b*. 1908), who was influenced by Jakobsonian linguistics in the 1950s and '60s, had a huge influence on European structural linguistics.[6] He emphasized 'structure' as the glue that holds together societies, for example as a kinship system. Language as such becomes a static structure that is comparable to the structure of a building. The task of linguistics was then to describe the various structures of the world's languages.[7] An extension of this theory was brought about via psychology. It was assumed that language structures are learnt behaviour. The notable proponent of language as behaviour was the American B. F. Skinner (1904–1990).[8] Chomsky was to repudiate his theory famously in his review of Skinner's work in 1959.[9]

How did Chomsky become a linguist in the first place? As the story goes, more by coincidence than by design.[10] In the first instance one might point to his father, a noted Hebrew scholar. In retrospect Chomsky must have benefited from his father's professional interest in language, even though Dr William Chomsky was more of a language teacher who also wrote a Hebrew grammar. Language teachers and language learners should not be confused with linguists, who study language *per se*. But Chomsky's father also did scholarly work on medieval and historical Hebrew grammar, with which Noam was familiar as a child before he ever heard of linguistics. When he was only about twelve he read his father's drafts of a study of a thirteenth-century Hebrew grammar, and later, while a Hebrew language teacher during his student days, no doubt used his father's textbooks, such as *How to Teach Hebrew in the Elementary Grades* (1946).

Growing up with English and Hebrew (the latter a second language), Chomsky also learned classical Arabic and basic French and German at university. None of these language skills, though, predetermined him to become a linguist.

Having drifted without a plan at the University of Pennsylvania, supporting his studies by teaching Hebrew at his father's school, Chomsky nearly dropped out. The turning-point, as he acknowledged in many of his early books on linguistics, came in 1947 when he met Zellig Harris in a political circle (actually unconnected with the university). As luck would have it, Professor Harris had the distinction of establishing the first department of linguistics at any university in the US, but it was not this that won over Chomsky to the study of linguistics within their first couple of meetings. In the first instance Harris impressed Chomsky by his politics, which more or less matched his stance at the time. As such Chomsky also listened to Harris's advice on his nearly stalled academic studies. He recommended courses in mathematics and philosophy, and mentioned in passing that he could also drop in on his lectures on linguistics. Chomsky responded with interest.

The group that met with Harris comprised a handful of graduate students. They did their academic work over a beer at the pub or at Harris's apartment, all in an unstructured way, but that still earned the students the necessary credits to gain their degrees. This freedom to work and learn was then as rare as it is today, and many a student would have been unable to respond, having been conditioned otherwise by an earlier public school straitjacket. For Chomsky, of course, this was a most welcome continuation of his early unorthodox, Deweyite schooling.

In time Chomsky became immersed in Harris's linguistics. As he read Harris's 1947 draft of *Methods in Structural Linguistics* (1951) he became truly caught up in the field of linguistics (Chomsky is acknowledged in the book's preface as having proofread the text).[11] At that stage Chomsky took for granted that procedural analysis along Harris's lines was the whole story. It was generally assumed at the time that the field was basically finished, apart from applying the methods to as many languages as possible. His courses with Harris were almost entirely an extension of the methods to longer discourses, since there was nothing more to say about the theory of sentences and their parts.

In 1948, when Chomsky was casting about for an honours' thesis, Harris suggested that he work on Hebrew. Chomsky found an Israeli informant, followed the field methods procedures, then started applying Harris's methods.

It was probably at this stage that the Chomskyan revolution started, for Chomsky started to question the methodology. He knew the answers to the questions, so why was he asking the informant? And the methods weren't yielding what he knew to be true of the language. There was no way, for example, that these methods might yield the basic root-vowel pattern structure of Semitic. So Chomsky started on what he took to be a private hobby, influenced in part by what he knew about historical Semitic linguistics, and also what just seemed to make sense.

The result was the first (1949) version of *Morphophonemics of Modern Hebrew*, with a rudimentary generative syntax, and a detailed morphophonemics, with a carefully worked out evaluation procedure and an effort to show that the grammar was a 'relative maximum' in terms of that measure: that is, any reordering of rules would make it worse. The rule ordering was quite deep, about thirty or so. That was heresy in structural linguistics. From then on, Chomsky was working on his own. He never discussed his research. The only faculty member who looked at the thesis was Hoenigswald, out of a sense of responsibility. Harris had no interest in it. Still, Chomsky also continued to work along the lines of Harris's methods, but by 1953, after years spent trying, and failing, to refine the methods so that they would work, he decided to forget the whole business and concentrate on generative grammar – his private hobby.

In the meantime one must reiterate that Chomsky's thesis was 'as different from structural linguistics as anything could be'.[12] With it he had sown the seeds of a revolutionary new approach to the study of language. The agenda was set for an investigation of the dynamics of language, how levels of representation transform and generate each other, and how the brain generates thought that generates language and vice versa. In addition any theory so postulated had to be tested against the praxis of language acquisition. In other words, we are moving from a description of language to an explanation of language.

Chomsky, in doing so, experienced the sheer delight of scientific discovery even if at this stage no one else was on his wavelength. Comparisons can be made to the young Einstein, who had a few sympathetic listeners when he expounded his revolutionary ideas but practically no one who fully understood the implications. Such self-contained genius can be hard to take at times, as illustrated by Einstein's response to a question regarding his reaction if measurements were to disprove his thesis: that the measurements would have been wrong. Chomsky too has this supreme confidence in his discoveries. He needs no verification by others, but it is welcome when it comes.

Having thus become fascinated by his own work, Chomsky entered graduate school at Pennsylvania University and in 1951 graduated with a master's thesis that was a revision of his BA thesis. He did it for his own entertainment entirely. Harris had his own consuming interests and, as far as Chomsky knew, didn't care one way or another about these matters. They were quite close, but their intellectual relationships were in other areas.

It was also at this stage that Chomsky became deeply immersed in philosophy, hence his eventual dual status as a linguist and philosopher. The philosopher who influenced him most was Nelson Goodman (1906–1998), both his teacher and later his good friend. Chomsky went to Harvard in 1951, mostly to study with the philosopher W. V. Quine (1908–2000), whose theories he would later denounce. Apart from these two, the greatest personal influence was the Oxford philosopher John Austin, who visited Harvard a number of times and whom Chomsky came to know quite well. Through Goodman and Quine, Chomsky was introduced to the work of Carnap, then of Russell, Frege and the early Wittgenstein. It was only fitting that Chomsky's first published academic text (in 1953) should appear, not in a linguistics journal, but in that icon of logical positivism, *The Journal of Symbolic Logic*. His article, 'Systems of Syntactic Analysis', sets the scene for the wider and interdisciplinary aspects of his research.

Notwithstanding his first publishing success and his highly idiosyncratic career so far, there seemed to be little prospect of advancement in academia or elsewhere for that matter. But Nelson Goodman, Chomsky's philosophy teacher, encouraged him to apply for a Harvard University Junior Fellowship. Such fellowships are designed for promising academic talent expected to do quality research that normally leads to a PhD. Chomsky was accepted; and the stipend provided was sufficient to live on. Fellow students

Morris Halle and Noam Chomsky, 1955.

included Morris Halle, with whom he would publish one of the great works in linguistics, namely *The Sound Pattern of English* (1968), and Eric Lenneberg (1921–1975), a psychologist who had fled Nazi Germany and who later taught psychology at Harvard Medical School. Lenneberg had a special interest in language and language acquisition as part of cognitive psychology. He was one of the first scientists of that era to propose that there was an innate language capacity situated in the brain. Chomsky, in a 2004 speech, notes that:

> the biolinguistic perspective, in its contemporary form, began to take shape half a century ago in discussions among a few graduate students at Harvard who were much influenced by developments in biology and mathematics in the early post war years, including work in ethology that was just coming to be known in the United States. One of them was Eric Lenneberg, whose seminal 1967 study *Biological Foundations of Language* remains a basic document of the field.[13]

Such an approach was in sharp contrast to the prevailing theories of the time, namely behaviourism. This foreshadows the now famous review Chomsky wrote in 1959 about B. F. Skinner's book *Verbal Behaviour* (1957), in which he demolished the notion of language as learned behaviour.

After a brief sojourn in Europe and Israel in 1953, Chomsky returned to Harvard and resumed his studies, with his fellowship extended until 1955. Apart from accumulating a vast amount of notes and ideas, he was none the wiser as to what would happen next. The only sure prospect was conscription: in April 1955 he received his draft notice. As he recalls in an interview with Samuel Hughes:

> I was 1-A. I was going to be drafted right away. I figured I'd try to get myself a six-week deferment until the middle of June, so I

applied for a PhD. I asked Harris and Goodman, who were still at Penn, if they would mind if I re-registered – I hadn't been registered at Penn in four years. I just handed in a chapter of what I was working on for a thesis, and they sent me some questions via mail, which I wrote inadequate answers to – that was my exams. I got a six-week deferment, and I got my PhD.[14]

That PhD got Chomsky out of military service. It is an enduring irony that militarists the world over seem to exclude the intelligentsia from active duty. On the other hand the ensuing work of academics is often supported and directed by the military and armaments industry. Typically Chomsky's first work at a lab (Research Lab of Electronics) was funded by the US's three armed services, as was most of MIT at the time.

Of more interest at this juncture is, however, the question of how Chomsky could come up with a PhD thesis at such short notice, notwithstanding the highly unorthodox procedures involved. Unbeknown to anyone, and in virtual isolation, during the previous months he had written up everything he knew – close to 1,000 pages. This monumental work was eventually published as *The Logical Structure of Linguistic Theory* (1975). Chomsky had taken one chapter from his research and submitted it as his thesis, 'Transformational Analysis'. It foreshadows a key concept that would revolutionize linguistics, namely that various 'deep structures' of linguistic representation (typically at sentence level) get 'transformed', by way of various rules, into 'surface structures'. A simplistic example would be the 'transformation' of an active sentence into a passive one. In English an active sentence like 'the cat ate the rat' contains many features of a deep structure that can be transformed into a less used (hence 'marked') passive sentence, 'the rat was eaten by the cat'. The sentence 'the cat ate the rat' is of course also at the level of the 'surface structure', but only a few transformations had to be effected to arrive at it from the deep structure. Deep structures could also be abstracted, especially as phrasal constituents. Hence the traditional subject-verb-object description of an active sentence like 'the cat ate the rat' was rendered as a tree structure (where s = sentence, NP = Noun Phrase, VP = Verb Phrase, Det = determiner, N = noun, V = verb):

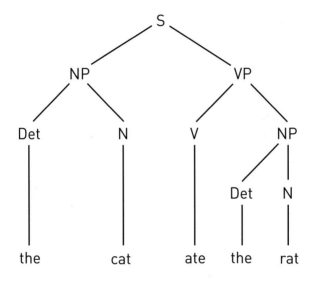

Another key concept inherent in this model is the binary branching, which assumes more and more importance as the model undergoes its numerous improvements. This type of tree diagram analysis is nowadays widely accepted and practised, even at the level of introductory linguistics for language teachers. It can all get horribly complicated when complex sentences are involved and when complex transformations are thus represented. Multiple pages can be taken up by a single such diagram. An alternative formalism, also popularized by Chomsky early on, was to represent sentence strings in bracketed form, analogous to the language of symbolic logic. The above sentence would thus be written as:

[s [NP[Det the][N cat]][VP[V ate][NP[Det the][N rat]]]]

As can be imagined, such an analysis sparked a vast amount of data, often concentrating on a single sentence and its type. Linguists would debate conflicting analyses and propose ever more sophisticated solutions to highly intricate problems. At this stage, however, Chomsky was only at the very beginning of that process. *The Logical Structure of Linguistic Theory* (LSLT) was microfilmed for the Harvard Libraries, and it soon became a sort of underground classic for the small circle of people in the know. Indeed much of Chomsky's work was published long after it had first appeared in manuscript form and been freely distributed among those who had an interest in it. Access to as yet unpublished materials creates a circle of insiders who are well advanced compared to those who have to wait for publication. That circle of insiders around Chomsky at MIT and a few other select institutions became legend and at times aroused a certain animosity among outsiders.

In 1955 the circle was very small indeed, and it still consisted mainly of a few graduate students. The one senior faculty member who became interested quite early was George Miller, one of the founders of cognitive psychology, then a professor at Harvard. He was perhaps the only faculty member anywhere who actually read LSLT, and he and Chomsky began to work together, publishing technical papers in mathematical linguistics. In 1957 Miller was teaching a summer session at Stanford and invited Chomsky to join him, so Chomsky and his wife and first child shared an otherwise empty fraternity house that summer with George Miller, his wife and two children: a story seldom heard in the world of academia. As noted before, another who understood Chomsky's linguistics was his fellow researcher Morris Halle, who already had a research position at the MIT electronics laboratory. Halle was at Harvard to do advanced studies under Roman Jakobson. This triangular relationship prompted Jakobson to arrange for Chomsky to be offered a research position at MIT. With typical self-effacement Chomsky has noted that, while he was made an assistant professor to work on a machine translation project at the MIT Research Laboratory of Electronics, he 'had no identifiable field or credentials in anything'.[15] Even worse, he told the project director that the project had 'no intellectual interest and was also pointless'.

His disdain for technology is based on his observation that much of it is simply brute force. In relation to computers and computational linguistics, he points out that computers can do precisely nothing unless directed by a program written by humans. Nevertheless he acknowledges that there may be some merit in computer applications and he retains a critical interest in the field. Actually the work Chomsky did in automata theory in the late 1950s and early '60s is quite well known in computer science. It was the basis for the Benjamin Franklin medal he received a few years ago, given for work in technology (including theoretical work, which was Chomsky's forte).The binary branching model of Chomskyan linguistic description is obviously well suited to the binary processing language in computers. As recently as 2005 Chomsky took part in a seminar on computational linguistics at MIT, where a paper was presented by a researcher entitled 'Modeling Linguistic Theory on a Computer: From GB to Minimalism' – where GB and Minimalism stand for Chomsky's theories, as we shall see. Ironically perhaps, Chomsky is thus much cited in computational linguistics. Another example is Dougherty, who in 1994 published *Natural Language Computing*, with the telling subtitle 'An English Generative Grammar in Prolog', and in the introduction of which we are told 'that the main goal is to show the reader how to use the linguistics theory of Noam Chomsky . . . to represent some of the grammatical processes . . . on a computer'.[16] Such eventual advances, and the nowadays widely accepted tools of machine translation, pay tribute to Chomsky, even though he himself remains very sceptical.

Now that the 27-year-old Chomsky was established at MIT, the best centre for the applied sciences that the world has to offer, there was a real question as to what his purpose should be, given that applied science was the farthest thing from his mind. Since he was to devote half his time to teaching, there was some potential. Initially he coached PhD students for their language requirements, preparing them for their French and German exams. As this was a task not requiring great intellect – indeed the language requirements were later dropped– there was another lucky break in sight. The MIT academic calendar offered a course on language and philosophy. This had been largely dormant due to lack of suitable lecturers, but Chomsky took over and never looked back.

Teaching his very own mix of philosophy and linguistics, Chomsky soon accumulated a wealth of manuscripts and original lecture notes, which in turn became the basis for his immense publications record. His first book, *Syntactic Structures* (1957), is based on his notes for an undergraduate course at MIT for engineers, mathematicians and scientists. That's why so much of its early sections are devoted to Markov sources and finite automata, and to showing why they won't work – it was almost holy writ that they must work. Both Chomsky and Mouton, the book's Dutch publishers, became trademark names in linguistics. *Syntactic Structures* was not an immediate runaway success in terms of commercial sales, but it nevertheless eventually became a bestseller as a classic volume in contemporary linguistics. Every self-respecting linguist must have a copy on his/her bookshelf, even if it is never read or understood. Indeed *Syntactic Structures*, as all of Chomsky's publications in linguistics, is quite hard to read and understand as he takes no prisoners when it comes to technical complexity. Starting off with some innocent-sounding axiomatic statement like 'let us assume that x equals y+1', there is an avalanche of logical implications that necessitate the reader continually checking back to previous passages in order to follow the line of thought proposed by Chomsky. Infuriating his critics, Chomsky is not averse to amending the axioms if new data requires it. As this is a matter of course in the natural sciences, Chomsky to this day cannot understand what the fuss is all about. While hard-core linguists battled with the new concepts proposed in *Syntactic Structures*, Chomsky caught the public imagination with 'A Review of B. F. Skinner's *Verbal Behavior*', published in 1959 in the widely read linguistics journal *Language*. As mentioned earlier, the article deals with Skinner's model of language as learned behaviour. That behaviourism was a dubious theory – best suited to the advertising industry and propaganda – was clear to Chomsky from the start; his main aim was not to discredit Skinner but to prevent the theory gaining in credibility, especially in philosophy and linguistics (as in science in general). Hence, more importantly, this was an attack on another Harvard icon, the philosopher W. V. Quine, who had embraced aspects of behaviourism in his model of a naturalized philosophy, parading as scientific empiricism. As such Chomsky simply demonstrated that the theoretical constructs of behaviourism, namely stimulus, response, reinforcement and motivation, had neither rational nor empirical import, neither in linguistics nor in science. Such a sweeping dismissal aroused considerable controversy in the academic community. Many years later, the media was to latch on to the controversy by reviewing another of Skinner's books, *Beyond Freedom and Dignity* (1971), and bringing in Chomsky to refute the arguments it contained.

That Quine's philosophy is a major bugbear for Chomsky can be highlighted by a strange myth created around Chomsky's now famous sentence: 'Colorless green ideas sleep furiously.' No doubt aided by a photograph of Chomsky at a blackboard at MIT in 1959 with the sentence in question, there has been much speculation what this sentence is supposed to demonstrate, if anything. Given its Zen-like qualities – not at all envisaged by Chomsky – there have been numerous attempts to elevate Chomsky to lyrical heights, including one by the American poet John Hollander, who uses the line in a poem – dedicated to Chomsky – entitled

'Coiled Alizarine'. Three lines of the poem, including the 'Colorless
. . .' sentence, are given prominence in a book edited by Gilbert
Harman, entitled *On Noam Chomsky, Critical Essays* (1974). It is
instructive that this volume was one of the Modern Studies in
Philosophy Series, demonstrating that Chomsky had by then
made a huge impact on philosophy as well. Indeed the introduction
proclaims that 'nothing has had a greater impact on contemporary
philosophy than Chomsky's theory of language'.[17] Strangely enough,
since the main aim of the volume is to curtail Chomsky's influence,
there is a reprint of Quine's 1972 essay 'Methodological Reflections
on Current Linguistic Theory', which is a second reply to Chomsky's
earlier article on 'Quine's Empirical Assumptions' (1968). The whole
argument revolves around Chomsky's recognition that Quine is a
bigger fish to fry than Skinner, especially inasmuch as the former
has taken on behaviourism as part of his philosophy of empiricism.
Quine argues that language and meaning are best investigated at
their behavioural level. Any such analyses are obviously also a
product of language behaviour – the paradox of language investigating itself – and as a result there is no way of determining the
veracity of one analysis over another, as long as both account for
the language behaviour displayed. Quine finds Chomsky's position
absurd, nihilistic even, in that we could deduce an innate language
system that guides our language output. Quine finds it pointless to
abstract lexical items and make claims about abstract structures
they might be part of. For example, the Chomskyan notion that a
canonical sentence (s) is made up of a noun phrase (NP) and a verb
phrase (VP) is only interesting as the attempt to describe a language
behaviour but not account for or explain it as some sort of universal
and underlying principle. Quine holds that all elements of observ-
able language (as behaviour) have and convey meaning that cannot
be abstracted or atomized without adding a new layer of meaning.
This includes grammar. Each instance of a sentence or expression has
elements of grammar that add to the meaning of its constituents (as

Chomsky and his sentence.

made up of words). Now, here comes Chomsky's sentence 'Colorless green ideas sleep furiously' to illustrate Quine's fallacy, namely while the sentence has all the correct grammar – and all the words have their individual meaning – it is nevertheless meaningless. According to Chomsky, the sentence example was intended to refute the whole range of conventional assumptions about what is a grammatical sentence: (1) a meaningful sentence (Quine), (2) a sentence with content words inserted in a grammatical frame (structural linguists, Carnap), and (3) a string of words with a high statistical approximation to English texts (conventional then among psychologists and engineers). *Quod erat demonstrandum.*

The Chomsky–Quine issue concerns empiricism and rationalism. Quine, with his narrow focus on empiricism, denies what Chomsky says has always been the true course of natural science, namely the explanation of natural phenomena by way of rational abstracts, which in turn are not necessarily subject to empirical verification. Take the oft-quoted example of Newton's so-called discovery of gravity, which nicely explains the motions of our universe – but no one, neither Newton nor any person since, has come up with an empirical explanation of what exactly gravity is. Maybe one day we will find out. In the meantime it would be absurd to relegate Newton's 'idea' of gravity to the scrapheap of scientific endeavour. In the same way Quine and empiricists in general want to relegate Chomsky and rationalists in general to the scrapheap of all serious science and philosophy. The arguments occasionally take on quite an amusing, if not sarcastic, tone, especially when proving the point that the empiricists don't have a leg to stand on. Take the assertion that, just because we do not have any exact empirical notions on how thought and language emanates from the brain, we should dispense with the ideas of 'thought', 'language' and possibly with the idea of a 'brain' as well. One can even go a step further, as does Chomsky, and pronounce at least some strains of empiricism, such as behaviourism, as 'brainless' and indeed dangerous. Chomsky minces no words when he asks 'Is this science?', and then goes on to say:

> No, it's fraud. And then you say, OK, then why the interest in it? Answer: because it tells any concentration camp guard that he can do what his instincts tell him to do, but pretend to be a scientist at the same time. So that makes it good, because science is good, or neutral and so on.[18]

Chomsky also argues that Quine's 'empirical assumptions' reek of the extreme empiricism of the eighteenth-century Scottish philosopher David Hume, whom Russell dismissed as follows: 'he developed to its logical conclusion the empirical philosophy of Locke and Berkeley, and by making it self-consistent made it incredible.'[19] One should note, though, that in certain respects Chomsky does regard Hume as one of the greatest philosophers, especially as he held that in order to understand the mind we have to postulate principles that are a kind of 'animal instinct' – and as such support the tenets of Chomsky's biolinguistics. Such apparent ambiguities are typical of Chomsky, who is highly selective in his evaluation of philosophical and scientific theories: there is no need to dismiss a whole theory if in parts it is reasonable.

Chomsky thus engages in one of the key philosophical arguments of our time, batting for rationalism in no uncertain terms when he dismisses Quine and his ilk. Since language has always played a central part in philosophy, Chomsky is not about to give an inch when it comes to defending his patch, firing a heavy volley at Quine when saying that his 'use of the term "language" to refer to the "complex of present dispositions to verbal behaviour, in which speakers of the same language have perforce come to resemble one another", seems rather perverse.'[20]

As mentioned before, an issue Chomsky is always willing to discuss, within linguistics and the philosophy of science, is the question of whether a linguistic theory should have a 'psychological reality'. While it smacks of an empiricist angle, it nevertheless sounds like a fair question, especially as it was posed often among linguists when it comes to the 'reality' or otherwise of phonemes. These are abstract sound units of a given language, namely those sound units that impact on the meaning of words so made up. The extension of the argument is to ask if a grammar, in part or as a whole, should, or even must, reveal or assert itself in psychological testing or whatever the scientific tools of psychology may be. Chomsky, however, finds the question disingenuous and vacuous. First, if linguistics is part of psychology, as it may well be, then it would be an odd question to ask, much as one would ask whether the Freudian constructs of the *id*, *ego* and *superego* are psychologically real – or for that matter if the behaviourist constructs of stimulus and response are psychologically real. If linguistics and grammar on the other hand are not part of psychology, then the question is equally odd. 'Do chemical formulas have to have psychological reality', he asks. 'Do chemical formulas have to have a chemical reality',[21] he also asks, driving home the point.

By the 1960s Chomsky was issuing forth ever more sophisticated and technical treatises that baffled the general readership with their scientific rigour but which instilled a loyal following in those who kept up with the latest developments. The latter were often astounded by the ease with which they could communicate with him and discuss ideas that have an impact on what has by now become known as the Standard Theory. Even undergraduate students became active collaborators in the research agenda. The corridors of the MIT Linguistics Department became liberated zones for academic workers, where status and hierarchy were left behind. Graduate students and new faculty forged ahead with new ideas and amendments to the Standard Theory. The essence of this work was finally published in 1965 under the title of *Aspects of the Theory of Syntax*.[22] This remains one of the great published works in linguistics, even though Chomsky and his supporters have long since moved on and established quite a few more theories along the way. In the preface of *Aspects of the Theory of Syntax* Chomsky pays homage to his predecessors, such as Wilhelm von Humboldt and Panini, who led the charge for a generative grammar.

The third chapter deals with deep structures and grammatical transformations.[23] By way of an example it generates the following surface structure sentence:

The man who persuaded John to be examined by a specialist was fired.

Since the sentence features two subordinate clauses, we have three base or deep structure components from which we can assemble the surface structure sentence by applying various transformations – including two active–passive transformations. Informally the three base structures are (where items in square brackets indicate grammatical structure items):

(1) [o] [past] fire the [s'] man by [passive]
(2) the man [past] persuade John of [o] [s']
(3) a specialist [nom] examine John by [passive]

Note the 'zero' item [o] in (1), which indicates the missing (or elided) agent, that is 'someone' who fired the man, or in the [passive] transformation 'was fired by "someone"'. Such empty/dummy categories or trace elements became important features of deep structures. Note also that the [s'] items are the embedded clauses or sentences.

While this is only the briefest glimpse of a very complex theory to generate sentences – in any language for that matter – it suffices here to point out that a powerful tool of linguistic analysis was launched. Not only did it successfully generate sentences, but it also generated an enthusiastic following with intense debates about the often minute technicalities that determine a set of phrase structure rules. The followers, though, were still confined to a small circle of MIT workers, but slowly and surely the circle widened despite the best efforts of the establishment detractors to have them suppressed.

It was at this time in the 1960s that another project on which Chomsky had been working with his old friend and colleague Morris Halle came to fruition. They began to co-write a monumental work that was eventually published as *The Sound Pattern of English* (1968). Close to 500 pages long, it spells out just about everything there is to know about the sounds of English. Among the book reviews on Amazon.com is this one:

The Sound Pattern of English (known as '*SPE*') is the most complete study of the phonology of any language that has ever been undertaken. It is the last word on English stress, vowels, and consonants. It will also tell you everything you need to know about how to write phonological rules, covering complexities like parentheses, parenthesis-star, curly brackets, angled brackets, and everything else. Chomsky and Halle also tell us about their discovery of 'distinctive' 'features', which are the universal sound system of every language. We owe them a great debt of gratitude for this stunning achievement. 'spe' was Chomsky's last work on phonology, so you can see what a loss it was that he decided to switch to syntax.[24]

This was posted in 2001, some 33 years after the first publication. Note also the reader's lament that Chomsky was apparently lost to phonology after the event. That is not strictly true, as Chomsky and Halle to this day have always paid special attention to the phonological component of grammar. Indeed Chomsky in particular has always reserved a special interface for the phonological form (PF) of a sentence. Even more interestingly, he has always postulated that the conversion to PF is the final step in the generation of a sentence. This seems to go against the traditional idea that phonology (and phonetics) are at the beginning, followed by morphology, syntax and semantics. However, it seems common sense to maintain that, while all the rules of morphology, syntax and semantics are generated in the language capacity, which is situated in the brain, it is only the final step to convert all of this into a 'spoken' sentence that emanates from our mouth. For example, at the PF interface we can postulate that we 'delete' all the surplus elements from the sentence, such as empty categories and 'null' elements. There is even room for some pragmatics inasmuch as our speech-motor-system imposes certain constraints, such as having to take a breath every now and then, thus interrupting the flow of speech – which in its mental representation (sometimes called Logical Form or LF) has no such limits.

In 1970 the MIT Press launched *Linguistic Inquiry* (*LI*) under Samuel Jay Keyser. With Chomsky and the members of a 'Who's Who in Chomskyan linguistics' on the editorial board, there was a mistaken assumption that it was a ready-made vehicle for dissemination, without any editorial constraint on Chomsky and his colleagues. In time *Linguistic Inquiry* became one of the best-known linguistics journals in the world.

As Chomsky's books on linguistics began to sell well to a wider academic audience (as opposed to his difficulties in getting his political activist materials published), many an academic publisher began to sense a coup and anything written by Chomsky was snapped up. Later on this also applied to anything Chomsky said in public lectures on linguistics. Apart from the 1975 republication of his early work *The Logical Structure of Linguistic Theory*, there was never to be another book to equal the scope of *Sound Pattern of English* (1968) and the smaller *Aspects of the Theory of Syntax* (1965). As his talks, interviews, lectures and articles were now becoming instant publications, there appeared a new type of collected works, often edited by a third person, such as C. P. Otero or Luigi Rizzi. Also, whenever and wherever Chomsky went, he typically delivered three types of talks or lectures: one on hard-core linguistics, one on language and philosophy, and one on political activism. Interviewers often quizzed him on all three topics and subsequent transcripts were cut up and reassembled in publications of one sort or another. One such groundbreaking publication was *Language and Responsibility: Based on Interviews with Mitsou Ronat* (1979).

Chomsky's technical contributions to linguistics in the 1970s are much concerned with extending the Standard Theory, so much so that it became known as the Extended Standard Theory (EST). Inevitably, perhaps, it was succeeded by the Revised Extended Standard Theory (REST). Apart from the ever increasing number of strange acronyms, these developments grappled with the interface of the application of semantic rules, and a recognition that 'deep' structures might just be 'shallow'. In other words, a sentence might be generated at one level of representation only. Further revisions gave rise to the notion that movement of sentence constituents leave behind traces, and that individual constituents can have intermediate categories. The latter became known as the x-bar theory, that is by virtue of the notation of placing one or more bars over category x. For example, a noun (N) phrase 'the very fast car' is a double-bar $\bar{\bar{\text{N}}}$, 'very fast car' is a single-bar $\bar{\text{N}}$, and 'car' is N without a bar.[25] This type of analysis allows for various types of expansions of sentences and phrases without having to invent new names for branch nodes. Another innovation was the lexical hypothesis that assigned a mini-grammar to lexical items (based on a feature matrix), which would allow for lexical selection rules to apply. For example, the English verb 'bring' selects two noun phrases, one as a theme (or patient/undergoer) and one as topic (or agent). In traditional grammar these noun phrases were commonly known as object and subject respectively. Note the reversal of the order in REST: the verb first selects for the theme (traditional object) and then later for the topic (traditionally the subject). This seems to be a touch of common sense that has been obscured by traditional grammar, which always begins with the subject. One can test such assumptions by some ad hoc self-investigation: what is the association one has with the verb 'bring'? 'Bring what?' seems to be a natural response, and only later one asks for the 'subject', that is, 'who brought it?' Those who disagree might point out that, in English at least, one always starts with a subject as in 'he brought the food', hence the mental process of assembling this sentence should also start with the subject 'he'. Not so, argue Chomsky and generative grammarians. First there is evidence from child language acquisition that in English children first acquire the verb-theme (for verbs that have the theme-topic choices) syntactic constituent before they advance to the fully fledged topic-verb-theme syntax. Research in neuroscience also suggests that the brain does not necessarily compute strings from left to right (as in parsing a sentence) but has the capacity to assemble (and comprehend) backwards and indeed in any reasonable order. Clear evidence is also presented by some verb-initial languages that place the so-called subject last (i.e. after verb and object). Latin is famous for not having any particular word order as the morphology clearly fixes the structure of the sentence: we know what the theme (object) and topic (subject) is by virtue of their word inflections. Linguists have long argued if there is a natural or universal order of basic syntactical constituents, and questions of left-branching or right-branching have exercised the minds of many generative linguists in particular. As we shall see, the Revised Extended Standard Theory (REST) was soon laid to rest, with new and exciting theories being developed by Chomsky and others in the 1980s, '90s and now.

In the meantime, the 1970s also proved to be a fertile period for Chomsky's more philosophical enterprises. Having already discussed his claim on contemporary philosophy via his exchanges with the influential Harvard philosopher Quine, there was a flood of philosophical works, including an enlarged version of *Language and Mind* (1972) and the classic *Reflections on Language* (1975). The latter is a compilation of essays and lectures given at McMaster University in Ontario, in which he asks the time-honoured question 'Why study language?', and sets off to provide some intriguing answers. Neil Smith, an eminent British linguist who wrote a book on Chomsky's ideas and ideals, notes that this volume is important in elaborating on the mind's 'modularity'.[26] He credits Chomsky with providing 'a wealth of evidence that the language faculty does indeed constitute a separate module, akin in many respects to any other organ of the body.'[27] While neuroscience has not yet provided conclusive evidence to support such a claim, there are increasingly sophisticated experiments with results that point in this direction. For example, researchers from the Wellcome Department of Imaging Neuroscience in London have reported that children who grow up bilingual have a denser brain structure than monolingual children in parts of the cortex that are said to be responsible for fluency of speech.[28] As such, empirical science is confirming the rationalist deductions made by the likes of Chomsky. Indeed Chomsky makes the point in *Reflections on Language* that the tasks of empirical science and that of rationalist philosophy go hand in hand. All great scientists have been philosophers to a degree, and many a great philosopher has started out as a scientist/mathematician, Bertrand Russell being a notable example.

The early 1970s also saw a remarkable meeting between Chomsky and Foucault on Dutch television. Foucault as the modernist gay philosopher par excellence and Chomsky as the linguist cum straight philosopher would appear to be as different as chalk and cheese. There are some deep ironies involved. Chomsky as the supreme rationalist is deeply indebted to the French philosopher and scientist Descartes, so much so that Chomsky's whole enterprise is sometimes referred to as *Cartesian Linguistics* – indeed the

A discussion between Michel Foucault and Noam Chomsky on Dutch TV in 1971, moderated by Fons Elders.

title of a volume he published in 1966. There are other French antecedents, such as the Port-Royal school of linguistics and Ferdinand de Saussure, who pre-figured the essential Chomskyan dichotomy of *langue* versus *parole*. With such a pedigree it comes as a suprise that Chomsky has an almost absolute disdain for post-modern deconstructionist French philosophy, which has language at its core. There may be several explanations for this state of affairs. One is that post-modern French philosophy makes a strong claim on 'political critique', thus giving it the status of political activism. Marxist analysis, which underlies much of contemporary French philosophy and political activism, is anathema to Chomsky. Suffice to say here that Chomsky decries all obfuscation in political activism, calling for plain language and plain common sense when dealing with the lives of ordinary working people. According to Chomsky, the playful and highly idiosyncratic political discourse of French intellectuals, which is understood only in the salons of the elitist Left, is a betrayal of the working classes.

By the 1980s some of Chomsky's many students had become leading linguists in their own right and they could pursue Chomsky's linguistics programme with further expansions, revisions – even innovations. And Chomsky himself continued with a flurry of radical innovations. First to appear were the *Lectures on Government and Binding: The Pisa Lectures* (1981), often referred to by the acronym *GB*. The Italian linguist Luigi Rizzi, who had been an associate professor of linguistics at MIT, arranged Chomsky's visit and his lectures in Italy. Rizzi had done for Italian what Richard Kayne had done for French. Both linguists had shown that generative grammar does indeed apply to languages other than English – a suspicion sometimes raised, since hitherto much data had been based on English. Chomsky dismissed such suspicions as myths and pointed to his own early work on Hebrew, to G. H. Matthews's *Hidatsa Syntax* (1965), to Robert Lee's MIT dissertation, which was partly on Turkish, and most significantly to the arrival of Ken

Hale at MIT in the mid-1960s, who elevated MIT to a world centre of Australian and American Indian languages – all within the generative framework.

In his GB lectures Chomsky set forth a revolutionary departure from the previous model (REST), replacing a plethora of rules with simple but powerful principles that could account for much of the data. We have already heard of the x-bar theory, and now there was Move α (move alpha). The movement of constituents in transformations, especially in question formation (known as Wh-movement), had become so complex that at times it became impossible to follow the rules. If one could find an over-arching principle that accounted for all types of movement, then the day was saved. To do so Chomskyan linguists devised Move α, which allows for movement of any phrasal or lexical items as long as it involves substitution or adjunction. The technical details are still complex, as various other principles of GB intersect. Introducing now the Binding Theory, we have to have a look at anaphoric relations such as:

(a) John likes him
(b) John likes himself
(c) Bill thinks John likes him
(d) Bill thinks John likes himself

(examples based on Smith).[29] It seems clear that the instances of 'himself' can only refer to John, while the instances of 'him' cannot refer to John but rather to anyone else, including Bill. In other words 'himself' is bound to an antecedent while 'him' is free (i.e. not bound). Consider then the sentence

(e) The possibility that John might fail bothered him

where 'him' can indeed refer to John as well (note that we cannot replace 'him' with 'himself' in this context). Given that pronouns play a vital role in any language, this simple sounding principle of 'binding' accounts, in combination with other principles, for a whole host of phenomena that previously were difficult to capture in a unified way. Note also that 'himself' (in (d) above) cannot refer to Bill. This is due to a locality principle that says that 'binding' only applies to a local domain, that is it cannot jump across certain syntactic boundaries. The same applies to movements, that is Move α. Another crucial theory that evolved was the so-called Theta Theory (abbreviated as θ-theory, and derived from the 'th' in 'thematic'). It is a clever reworking of what in traditional grammar is generally known as (in)transitivity or valency. As we know in traditional parlance, a verb can be either intransitive (have only a subject) or it can be transitive (have a subject and object), or even ditransitive (subject, direct and indirect object). In Chomsky's new GB theory, which by now is really a collaborative effort involving many linguists, these thematic relationships between verb and arguments (noun phrases) are newly elaborated in terms of the verb selecting the number of nominal arguments it needs so as to generate a well-formed sentence. Since the terms 'subject' and 'object' have become difficult to define, especially across languages, there are new labels for them, namely topic (for subject) and 'theme' (for object) and 'agent' and 'patient', depending on the role these nominal arguments play. We know from English that the active-passive transformation of

(a) The cat ate the mouse.
(b) The mouse was eaten by the cat.

leaves the cat as 'agent' and the mouse as 'patient', regardless of the cat being the 'topic' in (a) and the mouse being the 'topic' in (b). In Government and Binding theory it is stipulated that each nominal argument bears one, and only one, theta-role, hence the selection of 'agent' and 'patient' as labels that do not change even if their position in the sentence changes. English as an accusative language has many verbs that are thus labelled 'accusative' because they typically have an agent as a subject. Given this scenario it is interesting to note that English also has un-accusative verbs, such as 'undergo', where the subject is the patient as in:

John underwent surgery.

Theta theory also accounts for so-called ergative languages, which have quite a different system of verbs, namely predominantly passive-like verbs whereby the patient is the subject and the agent is a kind of optional object. Take an example from the Polynesian language of Niue:

(a) *Kua kai he pusi e kuma.*
  T   eat ERG cat ABS rat
  The rat was eaten by the cat.

This is a canonical sentence in Niuean and the literal translation is best rendered in the English passive (Niuean does not have a passive construction). The agent in the above sentence, '*he pusi*' (the cat), is marked with an ergative case marker and can be optionally deleted to yield:

(b) *Kua kai e kuma.*
  The mouse was eaten.

Note that sentence (b) cannot mean 'the mouse was eating'. This is due to the fact that the Niuean verb '*kai*' (to eat) selects for theme (object) the agent, and for topic (subject) the patient. When the theme (object) is deleted optionally, the patient remains as topic (subject). If Niuean wants to express the equivalent of the English 'the mouse is eating', it will have to use a different verb that is intransitive and selects for agent as topic (subject). Parallel to accusative languages, ergative languages have some un-ergative verbs (or it can be argued that accusative languages have some ergative verbs, and ergative languages have some accusative verbs).

Finally we get to the 'government' of the Government and Binding theory. This again involves a clever reworking of what is known in traditional grammar as 'case'. Latin, for example, is famous for its complex system of cases: nominative, vocative, accusative, genitive, dative and ablative. (English retains some in the pronominal system, such as 'he' (nominative) and 'him' (accusative). While in structural and descriptive grammars 'case' is a feature of nouns depending on what structural role they play, GB goes a step further and asserts that, since it is the verb that selects its nominal arguments, it must also be the verb that 'governs' case. In other words, the verb assigns case to nouns it governs. The details of this operation are too complex to elaborate here, but this opens up a whole new way of looking at it. For example, one can now say that nouns (or noun phrases) must be 'licensed' by a case node somewhere in the derivation. Another highly evocative explanation is that each new binary pair of syntactic objects 'merges' (naturally known as operation MERGE) into a constituent and all its syntactic objects must be 'checked' against the principles given in GB, such as having satisfied the requirements of the 'government' theory.

Given the whole binary nature of derivations, there is another important process that has become part of the key of GB. This is the idea that the parameters of a language are fixed by making choices between binary features. This is a powerful explanatory tool that allows us to make quite fundamental decisions, for example as to what language we are speaking. A child growing up in Niue will have as input sufficient data that will decide whether or not Niuean is an accusative or ergative language. Once this fundamental parameter is fixed, the child will go on to fix further parameters until the whole set of language principles is applied and specific structures have been acquired. This unified approach has been labelled by Chomsky as 'principles and parameters' and constitutes one of the great advances in linguistics today. *GB* was further refined by Chomsky with his publication of *Barriers* (1986), a slim but highly technical *Linguistic Inquiry* monograph. In it he discusses possible 'barriers' to government and movement, noting that one might 'expect that one barrier suffices to block government, whereas more than one barrier inhibits movement, perhaps in a graded manner.'[30] As can be expected, it is a highly technical treatise that has baffled many a postgraduate student and fully fledged linguist alike, but as it already points in the direction of a further development, it is worthwhile pointing out one of the key issues covered. Non-lexical categories now also become syntactical projections as part of the x-bar theory. While we are familiar with NP (Noun Phrase), VP (Verb Phrase), PP (Prepositional Phrase) and the like, which open up lexical slots to be filled, we now have the more abstract Complementizer Phrase (CP) and IP, where I stands for the category of 'inflection', which includes tense, modals and agreement (case). In other words, when we start off with a verb at the beginning of a derivation, the verb projects various lexical categories and these non-lexical categories. Leaving aside the CP, the idea of the IP being a projection that governs various constituents along the tree of derivation is very interesting. It is perhaps the common sense realization that tense is a concept imposed on a sentence as a whole rather than being narrowly associated with the verb alone. The binary principle also gives rise to another common sense observation often obscured by traditional grammars, namely, as far as tense is concerned, there is the initial bifurcation of only past and non-past. The old trifurcation of past-present-future is thus an obfuscation that has plagued language learners for a long time. Many of today's English-as-a-second-language textbooks still begin their lessons with the 'present tense' as the basis for all tenses available in English. Any serious reflection will show that the 'present tense' is in fact a highly specialized tense that evades easy definition. Beginning with the simple past tense is the natural way to go: an insight thanks to *GB*, if not to common sense.

A flurry of publications in the 1980s confirmed Chomsky as a pre-eminent philosopher, naturally in the domain of language. Having already noted that he has never engaged in any sort of political philosophy, especially of the French contemporary sort, we must keep to the strict demarcation of philosophy and political activism for reasons also stated above. Naturally even a philosophy of language impinges on the actions of mankind, and Chomsky for one is always ready to point out that our language capacity is the ultimate tool to change the world and make it a better place. Still, as he points out in his seminal collection of philosophical essays *Rules and Representations* (1980), 'the study of acquisition of knowledge or of the interpretation of experience through the use of acquired knowledge still leaves open the question of the causation of behaviour, and more broadly, our ability to choose and decide what we will do.'[31] What is becoming a recurrent theme in Chomsky's system of ideas and ideals is also high-lighted again in *Rules and Representations*, namely the biological basis of language capacities. Trying his best to delimit the emerging idea of a specific science to be known as bio-linguistics, he resents being co-opted into the latest trend of the time, called cognitive linguistics, in which language is part of a wide-ranging cognitive apparatus – also acknowledged to have a biological basis. He says that 'one must deplore the common tendency to insist that the mechanisms of language must be special cases of "generalized learning strategies" or general cognitive mechanisms of some sort.'[32]

By the end of the 1980s Chomsky had become a global phenom-enon. The first major bibliography of his work, compiled by two Indian authors in 1984, listed more than 180 publications by him and double that number for publications about him.[33] A 2005 search on Amazon Books listed more than 600 items by, with or about

'Chomsky and Predicate' comic strip.

Chomsky. He has become the most cited living author of our time, and he is among the top ten authors of all time. His voice is heard in academia beyond linguistics and philosophy: from computer science to neuroscience, from anthropology to education, mathematics and literary criticism. If we include Chomsky's political activism then the boundaries become quite blurred, and it comes as no surprise that Chomsky is increasingly seen as enemy number one by those who inhabit that wide sphere of reactionary discourse and action.

Chomsky's critics in linguistics and philosophy have mainly been focused on the latter field (for example Chomsky vs. Quine), even though some commentators labelled arguments in the former as the 'linguistics wars'.[34] Chomsky saw the whole excitement merely as a healthy debate in linguistics. He uses much more forceful language in the realm of philosophy, as we have seen already. While we will allude to some of his more irrational critics in the field of political activism, there was one so-called affair, starting in late 1979 and stretching into the 1980s, that seemingly began as an academic exercise. A French academic named Faurisson was suspended on the grounds that his university would not defend him from violence after he privately published some monographs on gas chambers; he was later brought to trial for 'falsification of history' (a crime in France). Chomsky, together with 500 others, signed a petition in favour of freedom of expression to be applied to Faurisson. To put it more precisely, Chomsky pointed out that he rejects the Nazi–Stalinist doctrine that the state has the right to determine Historical Truth and punish deviation from it. This, and only this, was the issue at stake. In what was an early sign of 'political correctness' gone wrong, there was outrage from a confused Left and Right, all vilifying Chomsky as some sort of criminal. Chomsky protested that in no way did he subscribe to Faurisson's alleged anti-Semitism and Holocaust denial; he merely supported his right to freedom of expression. Chomsky's dictum is that one must engage with the issues and not with the man or woman professing them. Had more Germans engaged with the issues raised in Hitler's *Mein Kampf*, Hitler might not have come as far as he did. One cannot tackle an idea by removing the person holding it. It is thus somewhat surprising – Neil Smith in his book on Chomsky makes the same point [35] – that in Barsky's otherwise sympathetic biography of Chomsky it is noted that 'the Faurisson affair does tend to throw some of Chomsky's character flaws into relief'.[36]

As alluded to earlier, one key strand of Chomskyan linguistics to date is bio-linguistics. The program that implements this in detail is the so-called *Minimalist Program* (*MP*), named after the 1995 publication of the same title. While there had been earlier mentions of the term 'minimalist', one can begin by asking what the term is supposed to convey in relation to a linguistic program. Taking it in its literal sense one might assume that the whole theory has become 'minimal' in its range of application. Not so, its range is becoming wider but what is being minimized is the system of rules in favour of a few but powerful explanatory principles. What comes to the fore now is the implementation of the long considered 'principles and parameters' approach. While some of these 'principles' had been developed in *Government and Binding* (*GB*) theory, there was too much of an emphasis on stipulating rule systems that define such principles. A radical new approach demanded that such principles should be stripped down to the bare bones. Take, for example, all this labelling of a tree structure (or string notation) – is it really necessary? No, it isn't, and here comes 'bare phrase structure', where all we have are the syntactic objects but no more labelled constituents. If we apply the principle 'Move α', then all we do is to 'Move α' up or down unlabelled nodes. The following tree is an example of a bare tree structure of the Japanese sentence

John-wa nani-o kaimasita ka? (What did John buy?)

as proposed by the Minimalist Program linguist David Adger,[37] but with the constituent labelling deleted:

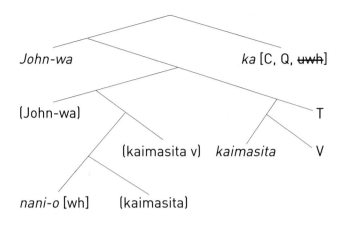

As can be seen, without delving into the technicalities, the verb *kaimasita* (to buy) gets shifted around quite a bit (indicated by round brackets), as does *John-wa*. There are two abstract (i.e. non-lexical) syntactic objects, namely т and v. Items within square brackets are features that need to be 'checked' – the strikethrough items indicate that this has been done successfully. An мр linguist can figure out what all the constituents are (i.e. the points where a branch meets), and in any case, since they are determined by the merged syntactic objects, there is no need to make them explicit and thus complicate the picture by inserting further categories. While for the uninitiated the tree structure derivation above is double Dutch, the figure still demonstrates the capacity of the *Minimalist Program*. It is the capacity to generate any well-formed sentence in any language, as well as being able to explain where and why an ill-formed (i.e. ungrammatical) sentence crashed in its derivation. Naturally all or most of the parameters of a given language must be known before such a derivation is contemplated, and in addition the principles applied may have to be modified to suit individual languages. The underlying skeleton, however, is provided by the *Minimalist Program* and the Universal Grammar (uɢ). The ensuing explanatory power is thus much advanced. No other current linguistic theory can make such sweeping claims. As Chomsky is always careful to say, 'if true', the *Minimalist Program* in combination with bio-linguistics and Universal Grammar shows the greatest promise in current linguistics research.

The net result of Chomsky's philosophy of language has been to wrest language away from philosophy and situate it within a natural science called linguistics. As for Chomsky the philosopher, what he has achieved in philosophical terms is to counter the claims made by Quine and other behaviourists, namely that language is learned behaviour. Chomsky's own counter-claim, based on his scientific investigations, is that the human language capacity is innate as part of a biological system. This nativist or innate theory of language has been the touchstone of both philosophers and linguists who subscribe to radically different ideas about language and mind, such as the *tabula rasa* notion that the mind is a blank slate at birth, to be filled only by experience. Chomsky's more particular theory that language competency is based on Universal Grammar (UG) has been questioned more by fellow linguists than by philosophers, but the issue is the same. Various schools of thought, such as functional and pragmatic linguistics, take much more store in communication as the driving force of language. Cognitive linguistics, although closer to Chomskyan linguistics, claims that language competency derives more directly from general cognitive functions, thus not stipulating a separate interface such as Chomsky's UG.

In particular, Chomsky's philosophy of language has made a great contribution to the age-old question as to how children acquire language and how they are able to use it creatively. No other theory has such an explanatory power. Chomsky has solved Plato's Problem for language, namely how come we know so much, based on so little input.

Hence, during the 1990s and up to 2005 Chomsky has merely reiterated his philosophical positions and has not contributed as such to the paradigm other than in his incarnation as a scientist *cum* linguist. In this respect he is very much like Russell, who, while popularly known as a philosopher, actually contributed very little to speculative philosophy. Russell's main contribution was in mathematics and, while mathematics has never been a sub-field of philosophy, Russell succeeded in demonstrating – Wittgenstein notwithstanding – that mathematical logic is embedded in natural language. Russell's popular philosophy – like that of Chomsky – is very much bound up in his political activism.

3
Political Activist

Anyone writing an essay on the rise of fascism and the fall of Barcelona during the Spanish Civil War must have a certain political bent. If you are aged ten at the time of writing such an essay you must be destined for a career of political dissident. Chomsky remembers

> what it was about because I remember what struck me. This was right after the fall of Barcelona, the Fascist forces had conquered Barcelona, and that was essentially the end of the Spanish Civil War. And the article was about the spread of fascism around Europe. So it started off by talking about Munich and Barcelona, and the spread of the Nazi power, fascist power, which was extremely frightening.[1]

A few years later his political education took on an added dimension:

> by the time I was old enough to get on a train by myself, I would go to New York for a weekend and stay with my aunt and uncle, and hang around at anarchist bookstores down around Union Square and Fourth Avenue. There were little bookstores with émigrés, really interesting people. To my mind they looked about ninety; they were maybe in their forties or something, who were very interested in young people. They wanted young people to come along, so they spent a lot of attention. Talking to these people was a real education.[2]

The uncle in question ran a news-stand that was a meeting place for intellectuals and professionals involved in psychoanalysis. Their political theories as to the state of the world were far more varied than the spectrum between traditional Left and Right. New York, as the great melting pot and first port of call for those escaping a bleak Europe and Asia, is a hotbed of political intrigue. While mainstream American politics is preoccupied with the difficult question of whether or not to engage in the coming military conflagration, there are, on the Left in particular, widely differing opinions as to what should or shouldn't be done. Young Chomsky's lessons in politics in New York were from a wide variety of sources, including those of the Jewish anarcho-syndicalists. They had looked to Barcelona as the promised land where a truly participatory democracy was on the verge of being realized. Chomsky's visits to the offices of the *Freie Arbeiter Stimme*, the Jewish anarcho-syndicalist news magazine in New York, yielded additional material. Although Chomsky did not know it then, Rudolf Rocker (1873–1958), an anarchist legend in his own time, was living in upstate New York and contributing articles to the *Freie Arbeiter Stimme*. Years later, an already politically informed Chomsky came across the writings of Rocker and cited him as an important source that informs his own political outlook.

While Rocker is just one of many influences on Chomsky, it is instructive to use him as an example. For a start, while Rocker was well known among Jewish anarchists, almost no one outside this circle knew about him – nor is he known any better today. Had Chomsky turned out a Marxist, Trotskyite, Maoist or a follower of Rosa Luxemburg, the traditional Left might have understood better his political activism. But Rudolf Rocker and anarcho-syndicalism? Rocker, in fact, is just one of the thousands of little-known activists who wrote large tracts on political theory and praxis, being revered by a small band of followers. Reading Rocker one gets the feeling of a boundless optimism as to where anarchism might take us, were it not for those ever-present obstacles in the way. He enthuses about the anarchists of Spain and Barcelona:

> the Anarcho-Syndicalist workers of Spain not only knew how to fight, but that they were also filled with the constructive ideas which are so necessary in the time of a real crisis. It is to the great merit of Libertarian Socialism in Spain that since the time of the First International it has trained the workers in that spirit which treasures freedom above all else and regards the intellectual independence of its adherents as the basis of its existence. It was the passive and lifeless attitude of the organised workers in other countries, who put up with the policy of non-intervention of their governments, that led to the defeat of the Spanish workers and peasants after a heroic struggle of more than two and one half years.[3]

One feature present in the writings of Rocker, as of the radical Left in general, is however the ever-present tendency to declare as Enemy Number One the other groups of the Left, instead of coming up with a united front against the real enemy, the Centre and the Right: Theodore Roosevelt had after all declared that 'anarchism is a crime against the whole human race'.[4] Instead Rocker rails against Marx and Engels, and against the perceived totalitarianism of the Russian soviet system saying that

> the idea of 'soviets' is a well defined expression of what we take to be social revolution, being an element belonging entirely to the constructive side of socialism. The origin of the notion of dictatorship is wholly bourgeois and, as such, has nothing to do with socialism. It is possible to harness the two terms together artificially, if it is so desired, but all one would get would be a very poor caricature of the original idea of soviets, amounting, as such, to a subversion of the basic notion of socialism.[5]

The end effect of such infighting seems to be that anyone outside the narrow spectrum of the anarchist position can be labelled a totalitarian. When, of course, the anarchists attack the centre in equal measures, the balance seems restored. When Chomsky does so, there is often utter disbelief and consternation from the centre and the left-of-centre liberals. How can he say that 'the US is a leading terrorist state'?[6]

In an upside-down world we may well ask how Chomsky deals with some of the other assumed bogeys of anarchism that instil so much fear in the heart of the bourgeoisie, for example the call for violent revolution or even the use of terror. Given that governments, corporations, churches, capital and property rule by violence and terror, the anarchist has the right to self-defence and if necessary use the very methods of the enemy, hence engage in counter-terror. These topics are hotly debated by anarchists themselves and indeed the 'anarchist terrorists' were often seen as marginal figures, 'isolated on the fringe of anarchist movements'.[7] Rocker – and Chomsky for that matter – do not subscribe to such violence, hoping instead that the enemies of the people will hang themselves with the ropes of oppression. Fat chance, as some might say. Nor does Rocker – and Chomsky for that matter – subscribe to the idea that the churches are part of the problem. This is of course again in sharp contrast to the Marxist position that declares religion as the opium of the people. While neither Rocker (as a Gentile) nor Chomsky is religious, they are willing to consider the more benign forms of religiosity as fitting with anarchist ideals. Chomsky is in favour of Liberation Theology in South America, as Rocker is in favour of a Jewish spirituality that has inspired Jewish artisans all over the world. Rocker was in favour of the Allies in the Second World War, a position that many an anarchist and leftist would have called revisionist.

It can be deduced from these examples that Rocker's brand of Jewish anarcho-syndicalism is just one position in the wide spectrum of anarchism, a splinter group within a splinter group. One may interpret this as the anarchist ideal in that every individual holds to his or her freedom, each representing a unique political perspective – if not a political party, so to speak.

That Chomsky would describe himself as an anarcho-syndicalist is simply a position that is derived from a scientific analysis of all available political theories, much in the same way that his linguistic position is that of a generative grammarian, based on an analysis of competing theories. Since political activism, however, is radically different from the concerns of science, there is one important aspect that Chomsky took from the anarchist position, namely that action is far more important than constructing theories. While the Left is littered with tomes of theoretical work that literally suffocate 'action' – as in contemporary France, for example – there is an almost spiritual call for action in Chomsky's political work. As a teenager he may have learnt valuable lessons from Jewish anarchists in New York, but he also learnt them from his home and school environment. While anarcho-syndicalism had great appeal from an idealistic point of view, there was much activist pragmatism practised by his parents and their associates in the field of education: to do what is possible – and not to live in a dream world of what is seemingly impossible – is the maxim. Change the world by applying common sense. Educate people for a better world by taking incremental steps. Change the system from within. No great theories are necessary to achieve this. Elsie Chomsky personified the gentle but firm approach in such matters. In one of her rare published essays she describes a drama lesson she taught:

> The first response to my suggestion was rather indifferent. The children assured me that the task was too great for them to cope with . . . I made no effort to minimize the difficulty of the work, but, at the same time, I convinced them that only such tasks were worthy of an intelligent and ambitious group. They were

quite easily persuaded that it was not wise to shirk a task because of its difficulty and to allow their inherent capabilities to suffer because of diffidence and timidity. The work began, and from its inception to the very last stage it was marked by a vivid interest, by unreserved cooperation from almost the entire class, by determination and persistence which no other activity had ever elicited.[8]

This type of work ethic and commonsensical approach to do good work must have influenced young Chomsky very deeply, even though as a teenager he may have rebelled, at least on the surface, by associating with the wilder members of Elsie's family in New York, especially with uncle Milton and the anarcho-syndicalists.

In essence this shows a young Chomsky who is already hard to pin down as to the single most important influence that makes him tick. As he grows older he adapts and adopts, but remains faithful to his basic principles. These are perhaps best summed up by the subtitle of Smith's book about Chomsky, namely 'ideas and ideals'.[9] Chomsky's ideals are thus rooted in anarcho-syndicalism, while his ideas for political activism are driven by common sense. Few people can understand what his ideals are, but many can follow what he expresses with common sense. His main vehicle for achieving this is through education – giving lessons for free – even though he is not averse to some direct action in joining protest marches and getting arrested or, in fact, organizing resistance, such as the national tax resistance in 1965 and founding RESIST, the main US resistance support organization from 1967.

As a young man, Chomsky behaved as the consummate political activist. For many years he merely pursued his ideals, poking around in libraries for anarchist and libertarian socialist literature, and becoming enamoured with Orwell and Russell in particular. While neither were hard-core anarchists, the former confirmed Chomsky's earlier take on Barcelona. Orwell's *Homage to Catalonia* left a deep impression on Chomsky, even though Orwell was not so much on the side of the anarchists. Orwell is of course the political activist *cum* author *par excellence*, the man with an upper-class education and a socialist heart. He had fought in Spain on the side of the POUM, the Marxist – but anti-Stalinist – Republican group, and had been part of the takeover in Barcelona by the orthodox communists, who declared both Orwell's POUM and the anarchists as 'fascists', hence as traitors to the cause. By then Orwell saw the Soviets as developing into a totalitarian state, a course of events later immortalized in *Animal Farm*. Chomsky was much amused by it, endorsing its fundamental message. As a historical footnote one might mention here that Orwell's main publisher, Warburg, also published Rocker's book on Barcelona and the anarchists in 1938.[10] There is a good chance that Orwell might have read it. Another connection between Orwell and Chomsky is the American political activist Dwight Macdonald, who published the political magazine *Politics* from 1944 to 1949 and to which Orwell made some contributions. Chomsky, as an undergraduate, was an avid reader of *Politics*.

For Chomsky, though, Bertrand Russell is next in line. Russell is a person whose life and work included much that should be greatly admired. He was first and foremost a scientist – a mathematician and logician to be precise – and a political activist second. He therefore embodies the scientist who has a social conscience and acts accordingly, very much in the way that Chomsky would develop. Both men have a conviction that in the natural sciences one cannot be a fraud for ever – one gets found out eventually. Empirical facts of nature cannot be obfuscated: a given theory proves to be right or wrong, at least as long as empirical measurements are part of the equation. The scientific mind is thus highly trained to solve problems and equations, using the scientific method, logic and (sometimes) intuition to try to answer questions of how nature

Bertrand Russell in California.

works. Such a finely tuned mind, when accompanied by a social conscience, is in a very good position to advise on problems facing mankind. Strangely enough, the human condition seems not to be subject to the laws of nature, inasmuch as science is unable to devise a method by which we can live in paradise or utopia, or at least in a socialist state of social justice. Chomsky's explanation is that the hard sciences keep to quite simple systems. When a system becomes too complex, physics hands it over to chemistry. The same thing happens for chemistry–biology, biology–psychology–human affairs – all far too complex to expect anything like the theories of extremely simple systems. That's why, since Galileo, physics has relied on experiments and idealizations, not what happens in the natural world surrounding the scientist. For Galileo and his successors, what mattered was what happens when a point-mass rolls down a frictionless true plane, something physically impossible, not what happens when a rock rolls down a hill or a feather drops to the ground, about which physics can say very little.

Marx, of course, declared that his brand of 'scientific' socialism would take care of that, but to date the situation has become, if anything, worse. Rocker and the anarchists long ago predicted the same, saying that Marx's scientific socialism was a betrayal of the earlier utopian socialism elaborated by Proudhon. Both Russell and Chomsky came to the conclusion that politics – or the organization of ordinary human life – must lie outside the realm of science, if only for the simple reason that the vast majority of ordinary people are not scientists. And as noted above, in the case of more complex systems, such as daily life, there are no laws for simple highly idealized systems that one can expect to apply. Both Russell and Chomsky therefore call upon 'common sense' as a basis to make the world a better place. For common sense to operate successfully there needs to be good information on which to base decisions. Here the scientific mind can be useful: to research and unearth good and truthful information. Common sense then dictates the appropriate actions to take. Since all ordinary people everywhere on earth are infused with common sense, much as people are born with a language capacity, there is only one thing to do: find out the truth and tell the people. This is what Russell did. This is what Chomsky was going to do as well. This is not to suggest a time line, however, for Chomsky had reached these conclusions well before he learned about Russell. As with Orwell, Russell was a welcome source of verification.

Another Russell–Chomsky parallel can be construed inasmuch as both are established scientists who cannot be ignored, unlike an unemployed, uneducated and wide-eyed anarchist. The establishment would simply eliminate the latter if he posed a real threat. One could not eliminate a Russell so easily – although one could imprison him, vilify and slander him, and deny him the right to teach. One cannot today eliminate Chomsky so easily. That both have tested the establishment to the limits is one of their great strengths, especially when they point out that the unemployed, uneducated, wide-eyed anarchist has far more common sense than any pseudo-liberal of the ruling classes.

When Russell wrote his 1918 book *Roads to Freedom*, subtitled 'Socialism, Anarchism and Syndicalism', he quoted Lao-Tzu lines of wisdom:

> production without possession
> action without self-assertion
> development without domination

One may note that Rocker's book *Anarchism and Anarcho-Syndicalism* has a chapter entitled 'History of Anarchist Philosophy from Lao-Tzu to Kropotkin'. We may therefore safely take Lao-Tzu's lines as programmatic for the brand of anarchism that Rocker, Russell and Chomsky subscribe to. Interestingly though, when Russell brought out a third edition of his *Roads to Freedom* in 1948, he distanced himself in the preface from his earlier approach to anarchism inasmuch as it affords too much freedom. Russell had become disillusioned about man's capability to be free, calling such wishful thinking 'wilful blindness'.[11] Chomsky, however, has remained the eternal optimist.

Chomsky's own road to freedom in the meantime received various setbacks as he attended first high school and then university. He had only known his Deweyite primary schooling, which in many ways was the type of libertarian Beacon Hill school that Russell had set up in England. High school, on the other hand, had a highly regulated and suffocating style of teaching, as was the norm of the day. As already noted, the same was true of university life in Philadelphia until he hit upon a couple of lecturers who combined science with common sense. These were his Arabic teacher Giorgio Levi Della Vida, 'an antifascist exile from Italy',[12] and Zellig Harris. The latter of course is credited with setting Chomsky on the path of linguistics by first impressing him with his politics. Both Harris and Della Vida were political activists, and they belong to the multitude of people who influenced Chomsky's ideals and his political ideas of action.

One should pause to consider Harris as a classic example of a general Jewish activism that is unique in the USA and, by extension, in Israel. One might classify the whole of Jewish history as 'activism' *par excellence*, and few would deny that the eventual establishment of the state of Israel is the outcome of a type of activism that is probably unrivalled in history. That Zellig Harris was active in the Jewish issues of the time is simply *de rigueur*. In his book on Chomsky, Barsky makes a detailed study of Zellig Harris and his extensive involvement in various Jewish movements.[13] A key issue promulgated by Harris and his group was that Arabs and Jews in Palestine should live together as one, that is, there should not be a separatist Jewish state. As we know now, this line of thinking had no effect on what actually happened. In a fit of Russellian disillusionment one might say that Harris's stance was 'wilful blindness', as much as anarchists are blinded by their calls for freedom. It would have taken many a Jewish Orwell to rush off to Palestine and fight for such a cause. In the event only those who believed in the opposite, a separate Zionist state, rushed there and fought tooth and nail – and the Arabs – to achieve it. That nothing has changed in this method to this very day is a continuing irritant for Chomsky, who still tries to sell the Zellig Harris solution. In fact things have become much worse: in Harris's time it was still a legitimate, albeit very unorthodox proposal; nowadays the same Chomsky line is generally regarded as a crazy betrayal of Jewish interests. Of course Chomsky remains optimistic, and every time he visits Israel he is encouraged by small bands of sympathizers who still agitate for a united Palestine, where both Arabs and Jews live together happily.

If they raise their voices too much they must fear for their lives though – if they are Arab, not Jewish. As it happens, Chomsky points out that such activism is tolerated in Israel to a greater degree than in the USA. Jewish dissidents in Israel are better off than dissidents in the West and face no threats, other than verbal abuse. Of course, if they refuse to serve in the occupied territories they will receive some punishment, but this is a tap on the wrist compared with what may face resisters in the US. Again, treatment of Jews and Arabs is radically different.

Chomsky, to his credit, is always very humble in the face of the real dangers people have to confront in places where oppression is more physical than legal. Still, the very idea of doing something outside one's professional interests is very much ingrained in Jewish professional and working-class tradition. Thus what must seem a natural way of doing things – that is to be a political activist – is a natural continuation of being Jewish in some way. Not that Chomsky sees it this way, after all he made a conscious decision, as we shall see, to be a political activist in addition to being a professional linguist. Zellig Harris may well have been the catalyst for both.

Chomsky joined the establishment in 1955 by virtue of being employed as an academic by MIT. Their ages placed Chomsky and his wife Carol in a peculiar situation. When the turbulent 1960s arrived they were too old to become hippies and too young to become establishment figures. They became something in between, occupying a somewhat uncomfortable middle ground, politically speaking.

In 1962, however, things changed dramatically when the US launched all-out war against the Viet Cong. Chomsky decided to become a political activist. It was a difficult decision as it would impact on his family life, make life generally uncomfortable, mean much additional work and travel, and it would alienate him from a hitherto sympathetic community of apolitical academics. He began to participate actively in the protest movement. He recalls that his first talks about the war were in churches or in someone's living room. Few people were interested: the primary audience consisted of the young mums and dads of the unionized Democrats. As is the mark of the true activist, this did not deter him in the least, indeed it encouraged him as he met with the salt of the earth. To educate one person is better than none. In fact it makes all the difference, as any good teacher will tell you. Later there were talks at colleges and universities, too, organized by the newly confident student bodies that increasingly became politicized.

Meanwhile Chomsky, as the dedicated academic, was always scrupulous to keep his politics out of his linguistics classrooms. This did not deter him from teaching some courses outside his departmental responsibilities. Teaming up with humanities lecturers, he would run informal classes dedicated to social and political issues. One such course was announced as 'Intellectuals and Social Change', another as 'Politics and Ideology'.[14] Luckily MIT did not stifle such seeming dissent, and Chomsky experienced no alienation from the faculty. They didn't agree, of course, with a few exceptions, but the prevailing atmosphere at MIT was real academic freedom. In fact, Chomsky was awarded a name professorship, later Institute Professorship, at the time of the most intense activism when he was carrying out activities that came quite close to being charged as treasonable offences.

As the 1960s came to resemble a roller-coaster ride, it even became fashionable among certain academics to declare one's left-wing credentials. To be a Marxist became cool. To be a Timothy Leary one had to go to Berkeley in California and do sit-ins, love-ins and tune in and drop out. While such hallucinational developments passed Chomsky by, he became increasingly sought after as a speaker for political events and demonstrations organized by fledgling movements that subscribed to the new phenomenon of people power. Chomsky recalls that his 'first big public event was in October 1965, on the Boston Common'.[15] He was to be a speaker but pro-war crowds attacked the demonstrators. The local media went into overdrive, denouncing the demonstration and Chomsky.

As the student protest movements of the 1960s took on a wider scope there was a curious delineation between them and Chomsky.

US Secretary of Defense Robert McNamara with a map of Vietnam at a 1965 press conference.

At least, it was curious to those who simply took Chomsky to be a protester, not realizing that he was also vehemently opposed to Soviet-style Marxism and its offshoots. Hence Chomsky did not become an icon for student protest, even though many a radical student protester took him to be a natural ally and flushed with excitement at the mere suggestion that Chomsky is some sort of anarchist. On the other hand, the establishment's fear that he was one of their own out to unmask the establishment from within appeared to make him a more potent enemy, precisely because Chomsky acted from a position of privilege – and when that happens things must be pretty serious. Not that Chomsky was alone: the now infamous list of political enemies compiled for President Nixon includes hundreds of such 'internal enemies', including Professors Chomsky and Galbraith, the latter teaching at Harvard.

One of the key developments in the formation of Chomsky's political activism was the meeting of minds with fellow activist Paul Lauter. Lauter

> worked for the American Friends Service Committee as director of Peace Studies and as Peace Education Secretary in the Chicago region. During that period he was also active in SDS, for which he wrote a Guide to CO. He was active in the Civil Rights movement in Chester and in Mississippi during the summers of 1964 and 1965, and with Friends of SNCC thereafter. He also was the executive of the US Servicemen's Fund, and was one of the founders – and for 14 years the Treasurer – of The Feminist Press.[16]

Together with fellow activists Hans Koning, Richard Ohmann and Wayne O'Neil, Lauter and Chomsky formed a group called RESIST. The current RESIST website tells us that the manifesto was

> published in 1967, signed by more than 20,000 individuals [but who did not become members of RESIST by simply signing the

pledge], and published in several public venues including *The New York Times Review of Books* and *The Nation*. The act of signing the 'call to resist' was a misdemeanor and those who signed risked criminal prosecution. The 'call to resist illegitimate authority' was used as state's evidence against several anti-war activists, including Benjamin Spock, Mitchell Goodman and William Sloane Coffin.'[17]

Article 9 of the manifesto against the Vietnam War reads:

> We call upon all men of good will to join us in this confrontation with immoral authority. Especially we call upon universities to fulfill their mission of enlightenment and religious organizations to honor their heritage of brotherhood. Now is the time to resist.[18]

Note the reasoned but uncompromising approach and the call for the pillars of society – universities and churches – to take up the cause. Note also how different this is to the approaches of the radical fringe student movement, which vowed to crush all pillars of society. Indeed, if these establishment groups had not actively voiced their deep concerns, the US governments of the day would have safely ignored the student voices. Not that RESIST was content with publishing manifestos: it became active in organizing actual resistance. Nor was RESIST the only organization involved in protest action. One event not directly organized by RESIST, for example, took place on 21 October 1967, when marchers outside the Pentagon were confronted by military police, who sprayed Mace and made arrests. Naturally there were no firm boundaries between organizers and organizations, many of which sprang up *ad hoc*.

Thus began a celebrated chapter in the history of political dissent in the USA, immortalized in *The Armies of the Night* by Norman Mailer, who was himself an active participant and spent a night in jail with Chomsky. Mailer's impression of Chomsky is recorded as 'Chomsky – by all odds a dedicated teacher – seemed uneasy at the thought of missing class on Monday',[19] and 'a slim sharp-featured man with an ascetic expression, and an air of gentle but moral integrity'. Chomsky, Mailer and others were released from jail the next day, but the state had to make an example. A grand jury indicted five protesters, none of them from RESIST, who seemed to have been selected according to peculiar criteria by the FBI. Indeed there was no indication that participation in the Pentagon protest had anything to do with the trials. It seems that the FBI picked people who had appeared at the press conference where the Call to Resist was announced, and who carried draft cards into the Justice Department at the time of the Pentagon March (that was real resistance, but separate from the Pentagon demonstration). Spock, Coffin, and Goodman satisfied both conditions – but Spock and Coffin had nothing to do with RESIST or resistance activities, and agreed to show up at the press conference mainly to help bring out the press. Chomsky was not chosen because he was on the steps of the Justice Department, giving a talk to the support demonstration, when the draft cards were brought in. Raskin was picked because they mixed him up with Art Waskow. Of the five chosen only Goodman was actually involved in the activities. The best-known individual of the so-called Boston Five who went to trial was Dr Benjamin Spock, author of *Baby and Child Care*. Spock was found guilty but was acquitted on appeal, as recorded by the controversial British activist Jessica Mitford in *The Trial of Dr Spock* (1969). In an interview Chomsky summed up the whole fiasco:

> The whole thing was like a comic opera. Ben Spock and Bill Coffin were asked to come every time we had a public event because they were visible and brought the press. They were quite happy to show up. The only reason I wasn't picked up was because, while everybody was walking into the Justice

Department with their draft cards, I was haranguing the crowd outside and couldn't go in with them. In fact, I was the guy who brought down the draft cards from Boston where they had been collected. But the FBI investigating was totally incompetent and couldn't figure any of this stuff out.[20]

As a political activist Chomsky also has the gift of writing up his activist talks and lectures, including voluminous research notes as a back-up: before long he had also become the activist writer whose books, articles and pamphlets reached a much wider audience than others of his persuasion. The first talk that anyone heard, outside the circle of activists, was given at Harvard in 1966 to, of all things, a meeting of Hillel, the Foundation for Jewish Campus Life; this was published in the *New York Book Review* a year later as 'Responsibility of Intellectuals'.[21] He was then asked in 1969 by Pantheon to publish his talks and articles in a book entitled *American Power and the New Mandarins*. Since it defines his entry as an important political commentator (and some would say political philosopher), we will pause to present the major ideas contained in this book, especially as it sets the scene for things to come.

The first of the eight essays in the book is 'Objectivity and Liberal Scholarship'. It introduces the reader to the 'new mandarins' in US foreign policy, those university-educated technocrats and policy advisers who, often in the guise of intellectuals and experts, advocate US intervention, by any means, in any country or region that defies US hegemony. In the aftermath liberal scholarship acts as apologist, evidenced especially in the 'deep-seated bias of liberal historians'.[22] That US foreign policy is essentially of the imperialist mode is demonstrated in the second essay, where Chomsky draws parallels between the Vietnam war and Japanese military expansion in China in the 1930s. The third and fourth chapters deal with the Vietnam war directly. Chomsky ridicules the US foreign policy obsession that the Viet Cong are part of the domino theory by which the evils of communism will roll back Western civilization. Indeed the very notion will force the Viet Cong to adopt Stalinist methods, thus US policy will shoot itself in the foot, as usual. That some American liberals, like Arthur Schlesinger, concede that US policy is wrong in its military aims, but correct in its moral stance, is also a bone of contention for Chomsky. This is putting the cart before the horse and thus expresses the fundamental malaise of US foreign policy. Chomsky maintains that 'the United States has no unilateral right to determine by force the course of development of the nations of the Third World'.[23] Among the remaining chapters is the article 'Responsibility of Intellectuals', which had been published earlier in the *New York Book Review*. Chomsky can be extremely scathing when it comes to so-called intellectuals of the Western World, denoting them as Stalinist commissars, frauds and liars. This may well be so in many cases, but there is little chance that the notion of the 'intellectual' will be dispensed with forthwith or become a dirty word. Ironically, just about every book about Chomsky touts the line that 'he is one of the leading intellectual figures of modern times'.[24]

In the last chapters of *American Power and the New Mandarins* (1969) Chomsky details what all of us, including intellectuals, must do to achieve a modicum of human value: to RESIST. Such resistance should be non-violent. Draft resistance is seen as a great example of that strategy. The book was selling well in the USA and abroad. *American Power and the New Mandarins* was in danger of succeeding as a subversive treatise that could affect the outcome of the Vietnam war. A year after publication Chomsky went to Hanoi as part of a group of anti-war activists, the others being Dick Fernandez (a minister in the United Church of Christ) and Doug Dowd (an economics professor at Cornell). Chomsky was invited specifically to lecture at the remains of the Polytechnic University in Hanoi, during a bombing halt, when people could come in from the countryside. He described it in detail in *At War with Asia* (1970).

Before going to Hanoi, Chomsky had spent a fair amount of time in refugee camps in Laos interviewing some of the thousands of people who had just been driven out of the Plain of Jars by the CIA mercenary army after years of intense bombing.

Since the US administration, however, was already well advanced in its plans to extricate itself from a war it could not win, it looked to so-called political extremists to provide an honourable reason for the defeat in Vietnam by claiming that the mighty USA was defeated, not by the external enemy, but by the internal one. Interestingly Chomsky holds the opposite view, outlined in his book *At War with Asia*, namely that the US had achieved all the major aims of its war and that the US corporate world pressured the administration to end the war.

Forms of internal repression in the US were mainly of the subtle but effective variety, such as COINTELPRO (an acronym of COUNTER INTELligence PROgram), an FBI programme aimed at investigating and disrupting dissident political organizations within the US. Given such repression at home, the US activists retreated into what they knew best: dissent by speaking out and writing. One of the champions of this activist genre was going from strength to strength: Noam Chomsky. The problem with dissemination was, of course, that the corporate media – chastened by the Vietnam experience – joined the internal repression and even put aside the commercial incentive that dissent, in its non-violent pacifist versions, sells well. Chomsky and some of his fellow activists were to dedicate considerable efforts to unmask the repressive propaganda machine that the American media and its international servants had become (discussed in chapter Four). Suffice to mention here that Chomsky and others had engendered an alternative co-operative publishing enterprise. Former MIT student president Mike Albert founded both the South End Press and, later, the on-line z Magazine. Both outlets published many Chomsky books and articles (and other forms of dissemination that arose with the Internet).[25]

One of the most vicious episodes of the Vietnam era was the bombing campaign in Cambodia, which President Nixon and his lieutenant Henry Kissinger began in 1969. Over a four-year period 539,129 tons of ordnance were dropped on the country, much of it in indiscriminate B-52 carpet-bombing raids (the tonnage is about three and a half times as great as that dropped on Japan during the Second World War). Up to 600,000 Cambodians died, and the raids were militarily ineffective, the CIA reporting that they served only to increase the popularity of the Khmer Rouge among the Cambodian population. The US corporate media did not report on the events – hence the campaign is known as the 'secret war' – but political activists knew exactly what was happening and were aghast. The unprecedented slaughter visited upon the people of Indochina provoked Chomsky and one of his collaborators, Edward S. Herman, to give a detailed account in a publication aptly named *Counter-Revolutionary Violence: Bloodbaths in Fact & Propaganda*. The book was ready for publication in 1973 but was blocked by a Warner Communications executive. Having had a look at the manuscript he was quoted as saying that it was 'a pack of lies, a scurrilous attack on respected Americans, undocumented, a publication unworthy of a serious publisher'.[26] While an updated and enlarged manuscript was finally published by South End Press, together with other material, as *The Political Economy of Human Rights* (1979), it is instructive to quote from the original manuscript:

Even a cursory examination of recent history, however, suggests that concern over violence and bloodbaths in Washington (in Moscow and Peking as well) is highly selective. Some bloodbaths seem to be looked upon as 'benign' or even positive and constructive; only very particular ones are given publicity and regarded as heinous and deserving of indignation. For example, after the CIA-sponsored right-wing coup in Cambodia in March 1970, Lon Nol quickly organized a pogrom-bloodbath against local Vietnamese in an effort to gain peasant support. Estimates of the numbers of victims of this slaughter range upward from 5000 and grisly reports and photographs of bodies floating down rivers were filed by western correspondents. The United States and its client government in Saigon invaded Cambodia shortly thereafter, but not to stop the bloodbath or avenge its victims; on the contrary, these forces moved in to support the organizers of the slaughter, who were on the verge of being overthrown.[27]

As we shall see in more detail in chapter Four, Chomsky and Herman embarked on a particular form of critique that unmasked the role of the mainstream media as a propaganda tool to make 'bloodbaths' benign when perpetrated by the US, and to portray them as malignant when perpetrated by the acclaimed enemy. Indeed much of Chomsky's political activism takes on this perspective.

In terms of publishing his dissident materials, Chomsky had as little access to the mainstream media as before. The one exception was the *New York Review* between 1967 and about 1973, but that had little to do with Chomsky, since just about everyone on the Left was in on it. Only Pantheon had kept faith with Chomsky. For European editions there was Fontana, bringing out editions of books published by Pantheon in the US. As such Fontana helped to popularize Chomsky in Europe, bringing out in quick succession *At War with Asia* (1971), *The Backroom Boys* (1973), *For Reasons of State* (1973) and *Peace in the Middle East?* (1975).

In *For Reasons of State*, the essay 'Notes on Anarchism' clearly restates Chomsky's position on what does and what does not conform to his brand of anarcho-syndicalism. While he insists that every new generation must, as it were, generate its own social theory and praxis so as to be able to respond to new developments, there is a long succession of thought and action upon which we can build our contemporary stance. As such Chomsky approvingly cites a long list of social activists from the past, including (in no particular order) Rocker, Bakunin, Guérin, Santillan, Pelloutier, Buber, Humboldt, the early Marx, Proudhon, Fourier, de Tocqueville, Pannekoek, Paul, Fischer and Souchy. Anyone who really wants to understand Chomsky should make an effort to consult the works of some, if not all, of these authors. As a mere indication, the following is a list – however incomplete – of some of the key anarcho-syndicalist ideas endorsed or formulated by Chomsky:

For the anarchist, freedom is not an abstract philosophical concept, but the vital concrete possibility for every human being to bring to full development all the powers, capacities, and talents with which nature has endowed him, and turn them to social account. The less this natural development of man is influenced by ecclesiastical or political guardianship, the more efficient and harmonious will human personality become, the more will it become the measure of the intellectual culture of the society in which it has grown. (Rocker)[28]

Anarcho-syndicalists are convinced that a Socialist economic order cannot be created by the decrees and statutes of a government, but only by the solidaric collaboration of the workers with hand and brain in each special branch of production; that is, through the taking over of the management of all plants by the producers themselves under such form that the separate groups, plants, and branches of industry are independent members of the general economic organism and systematically carry on production and the distribution of the products in the interest of the community on the basis of free mutual agreements. (Rocker)[29]

The suppression of the State cannot be a languid affair; it must be the task of the Revolution to finish with the State. Either the Revolution gives social wealth to the producers, in which case the producers organize themselves for due collective distribution and the State has nothing to do; or the Revolution does not give social wealth to the producers, in which case the Revolution has been a lie and the State would continue. (Santillan)[30]

I am a fanatic lover of liberty, considering it as the unique condition under which intelligence, dignity and human happiness can develop and grow; not the purely formal liberty conceded, measured out and regulated by the State, an eternal lie which in reality represents nothing more than the privilege of some founded on the slavery of the rest. (Bakunin)[31]

It is true that classical libertarian thought is opposed to state intervention in social life, as a consequence of deeper assumptions about the human need for liberty, diversity, and free association. On the same assumptions, capitalist relations of production, wage labor, competitiveness, the ideology of 'possessive individualism' – all must be regarded as fundamentally antihuman. Libertarian socialism is properly to be regarded as the inheritor of the liberal ideals of the Enlightenment. (Chomsky)[32]

Every anarchist is a socialist but not every socialist is necessarily an anarchist. (Fischer)[33]

A consistent anarchist must oppose private ownership of the means of production and the wage slavery which is a component of this system, as incompatible with the principle that labor must be freely undertaken and under the control of the producer. (Chomsky)[34]

The civilization and justice of bourgeois order comes out in its lurid light whenever the slaves and drudges of that order rise against their masters. Then this civilization and justice stand forth as undisguised savagery and lawless revenge . . . the infernal deeds of the soldiery reflect the innate spirit of that civilization of which they are the mercenary vindicators . . . The bourgeoisie of the whole world, which looks complacently upon the wholesale massacre after the battle, is convulsed by horror at the destruction of brick and mortar. (Marx)[35]

The dominant ideologies have been those of state socialism or state capitalism (of increasingly militarized character in the United States). (Chomsky)[36]

The problem of 'freeing man from the curse of economic exploitation and political and social enslavement' remains the problem of our time. As long as this is so, the doctrines and the revolutionary practice of libertarian socialism will serve as an inspiration and guide. (Chomsky)[37]

The Reagan presidency of the 1980s gave no grounds for optimism. Here we highlight the US foreign policy disaster in Central America and Chomsky's responses. Policies from the previous decade towards Latin America, especially Allende's assassination in 1973 in Chile and Kissinger's quip that 'I don't see why we need to stand by and watch a country go communist due to the irresponsibility of its people',[38] found new resonance in Reagan's administration, which held that evil communists, socialists and anarchists were assembling in Nicaragua and El Salvador. A band of fascist Contras was trained and equipped by the CIA, under the personal responsibility of Colonel Oliver North, Reagan's minion in such matters. Their mission was to search and destroy anything that appeared to pertain to an evil Sandinista empire, including Catholic liberation theologians and nuns who might stand in the way. As usual the US administration was shooting itself in the foot, but not before it inflicted pain and suffering on a small Central American population on a scale never seen before.

To Chomsky's credit, he not only raised his voice in protest, but during the 1980s travelled to the hotspots to support the people and organizations that battled for freedom and a better life in Nicaragua and El Salvador. At the time Managua was a refuge for writers, priests, human rights activists and others who could not survive in their own countries because of the US-backed state terrorist atrocities, rather as Paris was in the 1930s. Meeting with a wide range of groups and workers' organizations in Managua to discuss the situation on the ground, Chomsky also managed to deliver linguistics lectures at the local university in the mornings and public lectures on politics and power in the afternoon. One such major event was in 1985, when, over a week, he delivered a series of talks that were published by South End Press as *On Power and Ideology: The Managua Lectures* (1987). The morning lectures were published by MIT Press as *Language and Problems of Knowledge: The Managua Lectures.*

Chomsky had, of course, written many articles on Central America before 1985, but *The Managua Lectures* caught the imagination of political activists like no other. By 1986 Daniel Ortega had been president of Nicaragua for just two years and Reagan had responded by describing the Nicaraguan Contras as 'freedom fighters', comparing them to America's founding fathers. Reagan also initiated economic sanctions against Nicaragua. In 1986 a plane carrying US military supplies to the Contras was shot down and the only American survivor was captured. The US government announced that, contrary to the congressional Boland Amendment, the US had been providing military aid to the Contras. The supplies had been purchased with funds diverted from the sale of US arms to Iran. The covert operation became known as the Iran-Contra affair.[39]

This operation and the multitude of other affairs perpetrated by the Reagan administration to 'root out evil' in Nicaragua were rich pickings for Chomsky and any activist with an interest in such matters. In *The Managua Lectures* Chomsky reiterates the basic principle of US foreign policy as:

> designed to create and maintain an international order in which US-based business can prosper, a world of 'open societies,' meaning societies that are open to profitable investment, to expansion of export markets and transfer of capital, and to exploitation of human and material resources on the part of US corporations and their local affiliates. 'Open societies,' in the true meaning of the term, are societies that are open to US economic penetration and political control.[40]

What with Daniel Ortega and his henchmen wanting to close the door a bit, the Kissinger doctrine had to kick in. The metaphor of the 'open society' is still very much in use today, with the Orwellian tinge of carrying the opposite meaning of the literal one. That President Bush in 2005 wanted to confer the benefits of an 'open society' on the 'axis of evil' (Iraq, Iran and North Korea) is no great surprise, given that these are 'closed societies', as defined by US foreign policy. Having a 'closed society' on the doorstep of the US – in the shape of a recalcitrant Cuba – has long been an obsession with the US State Department, hence any signs of other Latin American doorstep nations following suit must be prevented at all cost. Even the tiny island nation of Grenada had to be invaded in 1983. In Nicaragua in 1985 Chomsky was thus reduced to tears of shame at being a US citizen:

> It is quite impossible for any visitor from the United States to speak about this matter without pain and deep regret, without shame over our inability to bring other US citizens to comprehend the meaning and truth of Simon Bolivar's statement, over 150 years ago, that 'the United States seems destined to plague and torment the continent in the name of freedom'; and over

our inability to bring an end to the torture of Nicaragua, and not Nicaragua alone, which our country has taken as its historical vocation for over a century, and pursues with renewed dedication today.[41]

Here a very realistic Chomsky voices his frustration and shame at his own inability to change the course of events. Did the likes of Allende (Chile), Ortega (Nicaragua) and Bishop (Grenada) stand a chance? Now in 2006 will Hugo Chavez (Venezuela) and Lula de Silva (Brazil) fare any better? Possibly one reason the US hasn't yet successfully invaded Cuba is that Cuba serves as a convenient bogey man for the US public, keeping at fever pitch the continuous portrayal of a deadly enemy at the doorstep of an ever so vulnerable 'open society', which must do everything possible to keep the terrorists out, including, of course, preventative strikes.

One of the themes inherent in all Latin American life and politics is the Catholic Church and its role in it. Many a political activist of an anti-religious persuasion might pronounce the Catholic Church in particular part of the problem. Even Rocker held that 'the less . . . that man is influenced by ecclesiastical or political guardianship, the more efficient and harmonious will human personality become'. Thus it might come as bit of a surprise that Chomsky has few anti-religious sentiments. In fact, for the most part he sees the Catholic Church in Latin America as part of the solution. A provocative-sounding essay published in 1979, 'The Nazi Parallel: The National Security State and the Churches', suggests that Latin American churches – Brazilian ones in particular – oppose fascism in a manner similar to the German churches that opposed Nazism. Chomsky (and his co-author Herman) claim that 'the most powerful bases of organized resistance in Nazi Germany were the churches, which provided the "most active, most effective, and most consistent" opposition to Nazi terror.'[42] This is a controversial claim in that the Vatican and Catholic Church of Germany under the Nazis more often than not collaborated with the Nazis. Under Article 16 of the infamous 1933 Concordat, German Catholic bishops were required to swear that 'in the performance of my spiritual office and in my solicitude for the welfare and the interests of the German Reich, I will endeavour to avoid all detrimental acts which might endanger it.'[43] The British historian John Cornwell wrote a scathing account of the whole saga in *Hitler's Pope* (2000). It is true that the Protestant churches were more proactive in their opposition to Hitler, but they too buckled under the strain. In line with Chomsky, though, one has to admit that the Latin American exponents of Liberation Theology are a totally different kettle of fish, and sometimes come close to what are the basic tenets of radical Marxism or indeed anarcho-syndicalism; as such they are a phenomenon quite outside the norm. With the election of Pope John Paul II in 1978, however, things took a turn for the worse. Barry Healy from the Australian Green Left summed it up as follows:

Pope John XXIII, who preceded Wojtya [John Paul II] as head of the Church by two papacies, is still revered by many Catholics for radically reorienting the church by convening the Vatican II Council, which directly fed the growth of what is known as 'liberation theology'. From Vatican II the democratic notion emerged that the whole church – laity and clergy – were united as the 'People of God'. John Paul II's pontificate was organised as a conscious counter-revolution against Vatican II – a winding back of the clock towards an archaic Catholicism politically aligned with violent terror against liberationists around the world.[44]

So perhaps there was a brief window of Catholic resistance in Latin America, but it is hard to share Chomsky's optimism in these matters, especially when he and Herman consider that it cannot be over stressed that while the church increasingly calls for major social changes, the vast bulk of its efforts have been directed toward the protection of the most elemental human rights – to vote, to have the laws enforced without favour, to be free from physical abuse, and to be able to organize, assemble, and petition for betterment.[45]

If the all-powerful Catholic Church of Latin America had done any of that, the twentieth-century history of a largely German fascist-inspired Latin America might have been a better one, Nicaragua and El Salvador included. Chomsky would, however, reject such criticism by pointing out that liberation theology was not powerful enough to overcome state terror, run or backed by the most powerful country on earth – with the support of the Vatican. On occasion Chomsky puts all the blame on the US Government (USG), as in the following statement from the 1988 essay 'Central America: The Next Phase':

The US military attack against Nicaragua will no doubt continue, along with other measures to restore Nicaragua to the 'Central American mode' and to compel it to adhere to 'regional standards' as demanded by *Washington Post* editors and other doves. Ideological warfare will enter a new phase. In the past, the task of the Free Press was to demonize the Sandinistas while extolling the terror states established and supported by the USG; to suppress Nicaragua's efforts to maintain a neutralist posture and the USG commitment to force it to become a Soviet client by barring aid from elsewhere and economic relations with the US, on which all of Central America relies; and to entrench the doctrine that the USG is seeking to establish democracy in Central America as it acted to destroy any possibility of meaningful democracy and social reform. This duty was performed with discipline and success. During the period of the demolition of the accords (August 1987–January 1988), the primary task was to focus them on Nicaragua so that the US clients can violate their terms with impunity, to suppress the US actions to undermine the accords, and to eliminate any verification apparatus so that these actions can continue. This goal too was achieved, a major USG victory.[46]

This is all fair comment, but perhaps fails to give any sense that there just might be some local collaborators with which the Americans work together. The Contras, after all, were mainly local thugs, and probably good Catholics as well. Again, unfair criticism, Chomsky would suggest, for would anyone object to a similar statement about Russia in Hungary or Afghanistan (or Nazi Germany in France and the Low Countries), even though the invaders had plenty of local collaborators? Every imperial war was in part a civil conflict in the country attacked.

Even if we subscribe to Chomsky's theory that all people deserve the benefit of the doubt and that it is the system that turns good people into bad ones, we are still left in a Catch-22 situation: we cannot get rid of all the fascists, who will never allow us to change or abolish the system. The role the churches play in this deadly game may well be benign and, on occasion, on the side of radical reformers, but as a pillar of the establishment and upholder of the dreaded system, especially in Latin America, again one has to question Chomsky's optimism in this regard. While Chomsky, having been brought up in Jewish orthodoxy, has found room to criticize very severely Jewish religious fanaticism as it extends into the political realm in Israel and elsewhere, he has failed to criticize Christian fundamentalism in equal measure, especially the abhorrent forms rife in the US. Here the paedophilia scandals within the Catholic Church in America should be mentioned, as well as influence that it exerts in Latin America owing to its financial clout. There have been recent reports that non-Catholic fundamentalist

Christian churches from the US are also having an impact on Latin America, as intensive neo-missionary campaigns are fought. There is even a linguistic aspect to that campaign, what with the Texas-based Summer Institute of Linguistics (SIL) translating the Bible into local languages and spreading the good news of US intervention.

Chomsky, however, maintains that he has on occasion harshly criticized the Christian fundamentalist right, and that he has never expressed any admiration for the Catholic Church, except when its activities merited admiration (liberation theology, for example). Be this as it may, there is so much more to Chomsky's political activism that deserves our attention: there is the central theme of Palestine and the Middle East (it's in his bones, as it were); then we focus on East Timor, which shows Chomsky as a dedicated campaigner for political and social justice for a far-removed corner of the earth; as a final topic in this chapter we feature Chomsky in the centre of the current maelstrom, 9/11 and the War on Terror.

PALESTINE. An ongoing catastrophe with which Chomsky has been closely associated as a political activist is, of course, Palestine and the Middle East, a struggle closely bound up with his personal life. He belongs to that minority of political activists who have come to the conclusion that Arabs (Palestinians) and Jews should live together in a single state in cooperation. In a concession to *Realpolitik*, he also considers the possibility of two states on equal terms. By 1974, as Chomsky has emphasized in his writings since then, Israel had lost the opportunity to establish a federal and ultimately binational state in *cis*-Jordan, and the only short-term option is the two-state international consensus that the US has blocked since it took shape in the mid-1970s.

These are admirable positions dictated by logic and humanitarian concern. The trouble is that most of the stakeholders have vastly different goals. Most Israelis fight tooth and claw to kick out the

Palestinians and keep them out. Most Palestinians fight to get back what they lost and to kick out the Israelis. A more optimistic reading would be that long ago the Palestinians supported the international consensus. A large number of Israelis do, too, and this is sometimes a majority, depending on how questions are formulated. But with American support and superior technology, the Israelis make sure that the statistics for collateral damage remain in Israel's favour, 3:1 at least. In his comments made in 1977 regarding American support for Israel, which still hold true today, Chomsky observed that 'there's been a very consistent US foreign policy in the Middle East, at least since the Second World War, whose primary concern has been to ensure that the energy reserves of the Middle East remain firmly under American control.'[47] Israel is the local sheriff and gatherer of intelligence. Israel also 'protected the "monarchical regimes" of Jordan and Saudi Arabia from "a militarily strong Egypt" in the 1960s, thus securing American interests in the major oil-producing regions.'[48]

How does Chomsky fare when he visits Israel and the occupied territories? It is certainly more dangerous than Nicaragua during the Sandinista versus Contra era: he risks life and limb in the occupied West Bank, breaking military curfews repeatedly. Pro-Palestinian American activists, such as Rachel Corrie, are sometimes killed by Israelis. In 2003 Corrie was run over by an Israeli bulldozer as she tried to stop it demolishing Palestinian homes. Chomsky's visit to the occupied territories in April 1988 was marked by quite a few close shaves with the Israeli authorities. He writes with cool detachment of one such incident, in an account first published in Israel in Hebrew:

> After the assassination of Abu Jihad, curfews were extended to new areas of the West Bank, among them the Kalandia refugee camp near Jerusalem. We were able to enter through a back road, not yet barricaded, and to spend about half an hour there

before being apprehended by Israeli troops. The town was silent, with no one in the streets apart from a funeral procession permitted by the army and a few young children who approached us, surely assuming we were Israelis, chanting the common slogan 'PLO, Israel No.' In the streets we found signs of recent demonstrations: metal remnants of the firing of 'rubber bullets,' a tear gas canister made by Federal Laboratories in Saltsburg Pennsylvania, with the warning, still legible, that it is for use only by 'trained personnel' and that fire, death or injury may result from improper use, a common occurrence. While we were being interrogated, a man who looked perhaps 90 years old hobbled out of a doorway with his hands outstretched, pleading that he was hungry. He was unceremoniously ordered back indoors. No one else was to be seen. The soldiers were primarily concerned that we might be journalists, and expelled us from the camp without incident.[49]

Chomsky's devotion to the subject of Israel and the Middle East is perhaps best expressed in *Fateful Triangle* (1983). In a foreword to the revised edition (1999), the eminent scholar Edward Said (1935–2003) wrote 'there is something deeply moving about a mind of such noble ideals repeatedly stirred on behalf of human suffering and injustice'. Chomsky's 'noble ideals' are tested to the limit in his unremitting denunciation of crimes against humanity. *Fateful Triangle* contains a staggering list of crimes committed (all previously unreported in the mainstream media, or at least under-reported), providing a carefully documented indictment that would serve any war crimes tribunal with irrefutable evidence. US foreign policy in the Middle East, as unleashed by its proxy, Israel, is at its most contemptible when it comes to the persecution of a war against civilians – women, children and the elderly. Consider the Israeli invasion of the Lebanon in 1982:

Again, it is useful to ask ourselves what the reaction would be in the United States if an Arab army had conquered half of Israel, leaving a trail of destruction in its path, sending all males to prison camps where they were beaten, murdered, humiliated, while their families were left to starve or be harassed or killed by terrorist bands armed by the conqueror.[50]

In few other publications is Chomsky as uncompromising and forthright in his condemnation of the atrocities of war visited upon Israel's neighbours. As we shall see, this spiral of violence led to even more worldwide calamities that have resulted in the present global 'war on terror', perhaps the ultimate chapter of an Orwellian nightmare where war is peace and peace is war.

The reactions to Chomsky's stance are extreme, as can be expected. As an American Jew, he is vilified like no other by those who call him anti-Semite, traitor and worse. But he gives as good as he takes when he rails against the right-wing Jewish communities in the US:

The Jewish community here is deeply totalitarian. They do not want democracy, they do not want freedom . . . the American Jewish community is their worst enemy, that it is a totalitarian community, that it does not want democracy in Israel, that it does not believe in democracy in Israel, that it does not believe in democracy here . . . they have a whole vilification apparatus which is pretty impressive . . . this vilification apparatus is really effective in shutting people up. It scares a lot of people off, especially people in exposed positions. There is just no way to respond. If you are denounced as being an anti-Semite, what are you going to say, I'm not an anti-Semite? Or if you are denounced as being in favor of the Holocaust, what are you going to say, I'm not in favor of the Holocaust? I mean you cannot win. Stalinist types of the ADL [the Anti-Defamation League in the USA] understand the beauty of throwing mud is that nobody can follow the details. You write it. Somebody else quotes it. Then somebody else says something. Why not say I am in favor of the Holocaust? I think all Jews should be killed. That is the next thing to say. The point is that they can say anything they want. It is a kind of status that the Communist Party had aspired to but never achieved. And they have achieved it. They are totalitarians.[51]

The ADL is the pre-eminent American Jewish organization that is supposed to guard against anti-Semitism in the world. In one of its publications Chomsky is referred to as a holocaust denier and a 'dupe of intellectual pride so overweening that he is incapable of making distinctions between totalitarian and democratic societies, between oppressors and victims.'[52] So much for a very brave Avram Noam Chomsky, doing battle in an arena that is very close to home, close to his heart. Too close perhaps, so let us move further afield.

EAST TIMOR. Indonesia invaded East Timor in 1975 with covert US approval. The US supplied 90 per cent of Indonesia's weapons. For Chomsky,

It is not easy to write with feigned calm and dispassion about the events that have been unfolding in East Timor. Horror and shame are compounded by the fact that the crimes are so familiar and could so easily have been terminated. That has been true ever since Indonesia invaded in December 1975, relying on US diplomatic support and arms – used illegally, but with secret authorization, and even new arms shipments sent under the cover of an official 'embargo.' There has been no need to threaten bombing or even sanctions. It would have sufficed for the US and its allies to withdraw their active participation, and to inform their close associates in the Indonesian military command that the atrocities must be terminated and the territory granted the right of self-determination that has been upheld by the United Nations and the International Court of Justice. We cannot undo the past, but we should at least be willing to recognize what we have done, and to face the moral responsibility of saving the remnants and providing ample reparations, a pathetic gesture of compensation for terrible crimes.[53]

Australia was a minor player in those days, but its role as the us's regional sheriff was indefensible. It was the only country to recognize East Timor as part of Indonesia, even though during the Second World War some 60,000 East Timorese had given their lives to fend off a Japanese invasion of Australia. In return for their treachery, the Australians gained important oil and gas concessions in the Sea of Timor from the Indonesians. In 1991 the brutal Indonesian oppression of the East Timorese independence movement was noticed by Western war correspondents. Two American journalists, Alan Nairn and Amy Goodman, were present at the 1991 Dili massacre, and Nairn testified before the us Senate Committee on Foreign Relations on 17 February 1992:

I saw the soldiers aiming and shooting people in the back, leaping bodies to hunt down those who were still standing. They executed schoolgirls, young men, old Timorese; the street was wet with blood, and the bodies were everywhere. As the soldiers were doing this, they were beating me and Amy [Goodman]; they took our cameras and our tape recorders and grabbed Amy by the hair and punched and kicked her in the face and in the stomach. When I put my body over her, they focused on my head. They fractured my skull with the butts of their m-16s. The soldiers put us on the pavement and trained their rifles at our heads. They were shouting, 'Politik! Politik!' We were shouting back, 'America! America!,' and I think that may have been the thing that saved us. They had taken my passport earlier but Amy showed them hers, and the soldiers seemed impressed when they realized that we were indeed from the States. We were, after all, citizens of the country that supplied them with M-16s.[54]

Such testimony made the American public wonder what was going on. As usual the mainstream media protested its innocence in not having informed the people: information was until then hard to come by. Not so! If the corporate media had published what Chomsky and Herman had been talking and writing about since the Indonesian invasion of 1975, there would have been no surprises. As usual it was in the interest of the corporate media to keep it covered up for as long as possible.

Chomsky was speaking about East Timor regularly from 1976 and writing about it within a year or two after that. The extensive discussion in the first volume of *Political Economy of Human Rights* (1979), co-written with Edward S. Herman, became well-known in Australia because it contained leaked national intelligence documents that had been banned from publication in Australia, and a mysterious fire then burned down the warehouse that held copies of the book. Chomsky also testified on the situation in East Timor at the UN Decolonization Commission in 1978 and 1979. That testimony was published, but not in the mainstream media, of course, although in the early 1980s he managed to get the *New York Times* to write an editorial and persuade the *Boston Globe* to publish the first good article on the topic in the US. Chomsky's book *Towards a New Cold War* (1982) also contains the basic data on East Timor, but without the background facts. He attended the first international conference on the East Timor crisis in Lisbon in 1979, and returned to Lisbon in the early 1980s to meet with East Timorese refugees. He also remained in close touch with the Australian support groups and refugees; indeed, most of his information was coming from Australian friends.

When Chomsky finally visited Australia, for nine days in 1995, it was at the invitation of the East-Timorese Relief Association (ETRA) and the National Council for East Timorese Resistance (CNRM). He gave several talks for them, including big meetings at town halls in Melbourne and Sydney. It was the first time the refugees had really appeared in public at meetings of this size. He also accompanied their representatives to meetings in Canberra and a talk at the Royal Press Club, which was broadcast live and rebroadcast several times over ABC nationally. An interview was also broadcast to Indonesia, thanks to the Rupert Murdoch media empire – unwittingly, no doubt. The talk in Canberra was a bitter denunciation of the treachery of the Australian government, particularly of Gareth Evans, the then Minister of Foreign Affairs. Together with the other talks Chomsky gave in Australia, it is published in *Powers and Prospects* (1996); the Australian edition has an introduction by Agio Pereira, head of ETRA.

The visit to Australia was closely followed by Alex Burns, an Australian journalist of the alternative media, who wrote an interesting piece entitled 'Operation Mindcrime: The Selling of Noam Chomsky'.[55] This offers some insights on the increasing media circus surrounding Chomsky, and what it means to be a journalist at the outer fringes of the media game. Burns first noted that

18 January 1995 was an extraordinary day for Sydney. Pope John Paul II arrived for the beatification of Mary MacKillop and the resulting media circus. Early morning commuters were greeted with an overcast sky and the news of a massive earthquake in Kobe, Japan. Microsoft's Bill Gates unveiled plans to dominate the Internet to business leaders. REM were scheduled to play at the Sydney Entertainment Centre later that evening. Virtually unnoticed, dissident Noam Chomsky slipped into this kaleidoscope for the beginning of a 3-city, 9-day tour. Sponsored by the East Timor Relief Association (ETRA) and the National Council for East

Timorese Resistance (CNRM), his tour started low-key, but became increasingly surreal as events unfolded at a fast pace.[56]

One should note that Pope John Paul II certainly did not use his visit to advance the cause of East Timorese independence, even though East Timor is heavily Catholic, and, second, that the media circus around the Pope was the real thing, not the one around Chomsky. Still in activist circles and among the chic New Left there might well have been an alternative media circus, if Burns is to be believed. One of his more cynical observations was about the audience responses after a talk given by Chomsky, saying that:

> after a five minute standing ovation, question time followed a similar pattern that I had noted before, where people ask generic questions that were virtually identical to those asked by the asinine media at the Canberra press conference. It degenerates into people attempting to impress Chomsky by asking smart questions that take two minutes, and emotional statements by local activists to promote their local causes.

Indeed such occasions do not allow for any genuine exchanges, however much Chomsky might want to facilitate it himself. Things get worse when the speaking engagements get mixed up by chaotic local operators, who attach 'minders' to Chomsky and whisk him from place to place. As Carol Chomsky, his minder in later years, has pointed out, in such situations Chomsky tends to agree to yet another unplanned speaking or interview situation and thus, quite unwittingly, disappoints those who have been waiting patiently at a planned/advertised venue, arriving hours late or never. Burns writes of one such occasion:

> By this time a crowd of twenty people had formed around Chomsky, thrusting microphones and cameras into his face as

he autographed books at a frantic pace. 'Who do you think assassinated Kennedy?', another voice asked. 'I've written a book on it, why don't you go and read that?' Chomsky was visibly seething and his voice betrayed a tired frustration at having to answer a question asked many times before. Flanked by minders, Chomsky was hurriedly escorted to another destination. Behind him lay a group of bitter writers, angry at not having had the opportunity to question him further. They were too busy arguing to realise that asking the right kind of question was just as important as asking any questions at all. Some were dismayed at coming face to face with their hero and having their rhetoric rebuffed and their 'commitment' shown to be shallow and reactionary. They were unable to separate the man from the myth. The activists were still locked into 'revolutionary techniques' that were outdated by the information revolution. The diehard journalists had attempted to gain interviews or only a few minutes of Chomsky's time, and whilst he was keen to speak to as many people as possible, his minders shielded him from direct contact in many cases.[57]

Burns and his fellow activists in Australia were certainly amazed to hear Chomsky say what few in his position would ever have said:

In terms of world affairs and international law this isn't a difficult situation to solve . . . This isn't Rwanda or Bosnia – we don't have to bomb Jakarta. What we need to do is withdraw from the Timor Gap Treaty, which seems to me to be offensive to decent human beings. The same government which signed the treaty in 1991 also revoked recognition of the Soviet control of the Baltic States. Australia led the way in formulating international laws protecting human rights, yet the ratified treaty with Indonesia is the only one to my knowledge that exists in the world that violates the principles you signed. According to a secret cable of August 1975, the Ambassador to Jakarta, Richard Woolcott, felt that 'we should take a pragmatic rather than a principled interest' in the impending invasion. He felt that a favourable treaty could be 'more easily negotiated with Indonesia . . . than with Portugal or an independent East Timor.' So we have East Timorese being slaughtered just so that an oil company can make a few more profits.[58]

As such Chomsky did more to advance the cause of the East Timorese than anyone, other than the investigative journalist John Pilger. Another contributory factor was the first screenings in Australia (from 1992) and elsewhere of the documentary film *Manufacturing Consent*, which was based on the book of the same title by Herman and Chomsky. The film covers the East Timor issue and Burns quotes the producer/director Mark Achbar as saying:

I think the film is in part responsible for the fact that a sentence came out of Chrétien's and Clinton's mouths about Indonesian human rights abuses at their last APEC meeting in Jakarta. When I was in Australia for the commercial opening of the film, two East Timorese refugees presented me with a ceremonial shawl and thanked Peter and I for getting their story right and for bringing it to the world. That meant more to me than any of the awards the film has won.[59]

A little-known story that involves East Timor and New Zealand also speaks volumes about Chomsky. In November 1991, three weeks after Kamal Bamadhaj, a twenty-year-old New Zealand-Malaysian student, had arrived in East Timor as a member of an Australian aid organization, he was shot in the back, fatally, by Indonesian military police. For four years Kamal's mother, journalist Helen Todd, crusaded to bring the perpetrators of the crime to justice. The New

Zealand government of the time was as cowardly as its Australian counterpart, and Helen Todd received no support whatsoever from the New Zealand authorities. Nonetheless her investigations revealed some of the Indonesian military officers in charge at the Dili massacre. Names were circulated among the international community of political activists and human rights campaigners, including that of one General Sintong Panjaitan. In 1994, with supreme impunity, the same general enrolled in a course at Harvard University. Since many of the top brass of the Indonesian armed forces had previously trained in the US, it was nothing unusual for the elite classes of both countries to have exchanges at all levels: to protect their immunity they simply adopted different names for the time being. Chomsky came to hear about this from East Timor activists, either there or perhaps in Australia; local activists in the Boston area then alerted the Harvard authorities. Of course the Harvard establishment at first denied all knowledge of such a connection, but positive proof soon led to pickets at the general's up-market house. News of these events reached Helen Todd in New Zealand. When the general was warned, most likely by the US government, that moves were underway to start US civil proceedings against him, he immediately left the country. Chomsky still relishes what he calls his favourite headline ever in the US press: 'Indonesian General Flees Boston'. With the assistance of a group of United States lawyers working for the Center for Constitutional Rights, including Chomsky's sister-in-law, Todd's quest ended in 1994 in a Boston courtroom, where, in a groundbreaking case, she successfully sued General Sintong Panjaitan – *in absentia*. Panjaitan was ordered to pay $NZ22 million, $NZ16 million of which was for Todd herself for punitive damages. The general called the ruling a joke and continues to refuse to pay. Chomsky has never met Helen Todd in person but communicated with her on many occasions during that period. A New Zealand Green Member of Parliament, Keith Locke, wrote in 1998:

Our Foreign Minister was also very 'diplomatic' in 1994, when a US court ordered the Indonesian general in charge during the massacre to pay Kamal's mother, Helen Todd, $32 million in punitive damages. Mr McKinnon agreed only to ask the Indonesians 'what they were doing about the judgement and if they are going to appeal against it.'[60]

The same Don McKinnon's present position (2005) as Secretary-General of the Commonwealth has given rise to the cynical observation that generals and ministers don't die, they just get recycled to different posts.

When public opinion in the US, Australia and New Zealand swung around in favour of East Timorese independence, or at least autonomy from Indonesia, all three governments took the moral high ground. It was opportune to do so, since the Suharto regime began to crumble in 1998 and soon some of the dirty deals he had made with the governments in question might be revealed. For almost ten years after the Dili massacre in 1991 all three governments had held Suharto's hand, but faced with the Islamist tendencies of his successor, Habibie, there would be a total reversal. The slaughter that followed the 1999 East Timorese vote for independence put US foreign policy under pressure and President Clinton withdrew support from the Indonesian military. They in turn withdrew immediately from East Timor and the Australian-led International Force in East Timor (INTERFET) landed unopposed on 20 September 1999. Lauded by the international mainstream media as a noble humanitarian intervention, Chomsky pours scorn on the claim, saying that 'there was no intervention, let alone humanitarian intervention'.[61] What really happened was that the US, as elsewhere in the world, had supported a gangster regime for too long and lost control of the chief gangster, in this case Suharto. It then had to close down the operation, leaving chaos all round. The East Timorese population paid the price – up to 100,000 lives. As Australia took control of the newly independent Timor-Leste, via its aid industry, there came another surprise, revealing, some might say, the height of duplicity and cynicism. The Australian government under John Howard demanded that Australian access to oil and gas under the 1989 Timor Gap Treaty, which had been negotiated with Indonesia as thanks for recognizing the legitimacy of the 1975 invasion, was to be renewed unchanged with Timor-Leste, providing vast access to Australian/US oil and gas companies. While negotiations drag on with no end in sight, East Timorese activists have a new battle on their hands:

> The Movement Against the Occupation of the Timor Sea was formed in Dili, Timor-Leste in April 2004 to help the Australian government and people better understand how people in Timor-Leste feel about Australia's violations of our rights, occupation of our maritime territory, theft of our resources, and denial of our nationhood . . . We want to make it clear to the general public and the press that this is a national movement that include[s] all levels of Timorese society where children, youth, women, the elderly, the poor and the needy are well represented.[62]

The independence East Timor achieved in May 2002 is a real tribute to the handful of, mostly young, East Timorese activists who, over a period of 25 years, devoted enormous energy and efforts to achieving it, and to their (considerably more numerous) counterparts in Australia and other countries throughout the West.

9/11 AND THE 'WAR ON TERROR'. When the world changed, as they say, on 11 September 2001, there was an incredible media frenzy to explain, to vilify, to call for revenge, to mitigate, to confuse, to replay the scene again and again, to opine, to investigate . . . across every shade of the political spectrum. Naturally, Chomsky was much in demand, and he gave many interviews in September and early October. Sadly perhaps, he was persuaded that a collection of these interviews should be published in a slim volume, entitled *September 11*, which was already in print by 15 October. He and many such others were caught in limbo. Chapter 7 of Chomsky's book is entitled 'Considerable Constraint?' (ironically with a question-mark). It appears that Chomsky and many others completely missed the point: for a minute Chomsky thought that Bush and Co. would indeed show constraint:

> From the first days after the attack, the Bush administration has been warned by NATO, specialists on the region, and presumably its own intelligence agencies (not to speak of many people like you and me) that if they react with a massive assault that kills many innocent people, they will be fulfilling the ardent wishes of bin Laden and others like him . . . The message appears to have finally gotten through to the Bush administration, which has – wisely from their point of view – chosen to follow a different course.[63]

Chomsky maintains that he was right in that the US did not respond as massively as they could have. It seems a moot point. The ensuing slaughter in Afghanistan – and as it continues to this day – cannot be dismissed. While any misjudgements of the situation can easily be excused by the resulting political confusion, that it should have happened to Chomsky in print was perhaps an avoidable misjudgement. Chomsky's *September 11* is thus an odd contribution to the history of events, knocked flat by some publicist's eagerness to cash in on the Chomsky phenomenon. Not that the collection of interviews is devoid of words of wisdom: Chomsky quotes a Mexican bishop who famously tells the Americans to 'reflect on why they are so hated, having generated so much violence to protect their economic interests'.[64] Of course the book was bitterly attacked because it didn't line up for the patriotic parade. Not surprisingly, though, *September 11* still proved to be a publishing success for New York-based Seven Stories Press, which was able to claim that 'Noam Chomsky's 9-11 became the single most influential counter-narrative of dissent, selling over 300,000 copies and was the #1 paperback in Canada throughout 2002.'[65]

While the world watched the fall of Kabul on CNN, with some alternative shots from the newly established Arab television stations such as Al Jazeera (but waited in vain for the scalp of Osama bin Laden), a new world order was introduced that sought to contain, once and for all, any resistance to US global dominance. On a roll in Afghanistan, here was an opportunity to subdue the remaining members of the 'axis of evil' as well, starting with Iraq and its extremely important oil reserves. This was the real *raison d'être* of US foreign policy, as Chomsky had pointed out over and over again for many years. Iraq, Iran and Syria must be taught a lesson and brought to heel. They must accept that their oil is to be pumped by American-dominated multinational corporations, cheaply and effectively, to maximize corporate profits that in turn purchase geopolitical power in Washington's armaments industry. The cynical charades played by Secretary of State Colen Powell to convince the world that Saddam Hussein, Washington's own man, had WMDs (interpreted by one wit as 'weapons of mass deception'), and so justifying the necessity to invade, are by now also history or, as Marx would say, 'history as farce'.

These events in Iraq, and all the other regional wars raging across the world, AIDS and poverty in Africa, turmoil in the former Soviet states, Russia's terror in Chechnya suddenly becoming a legitimate war on terror in league with the US and China, the whole world reeling in a merry-go-round of capitalist excess and luxury as the economic and political elites exploit anyone they can only intensifies Chomsky's commitment to political activism. Now in his seventies, he travels more than ever, gives more talks, writes more. Ever the optimist, he puts his faith in new peoples' movements, such as the World Social Forum, which he has attended in

Arundhati Roy and Chomsky at his 75th birthday celebration.

India and Brazil. His network of political activists widens as he travels the world. Increasingly activists associated with the World Social Forum, that is activists from the so-called Third World (or the South, as Willy Brandt had called it), turn to Chomsky as their comrade-in-arms. Good things happen. Chomsky has long known Luiz Inácio Lula da Silva as a good man, and now he is as President of Brazil. I ask Chomsky if Lula da Silva shouldn't have abolished the state of Brazil by now and introduced council communism or anarcho-syndicalist freedom. Chomsky answers that it's easy for us to say such things because we do not have to live with the consequences – Lula da Silva has to. I agree. In India Chomsky has teamed up with writer turned activist Arundhati Roy, who began a speech at the opening of the Mumbai World Social Forum on 16 January 2004 in the following brilliant fashion: 'Last January thousands of us from across the world gathered in Porto Alegre in Brazil and declared – reiterated – that "Another World Is Possible." A few thousand miles north, in Washington, George Bush and his aides were thinking the same thing.'[66]

The previous year Arundhati Roy had written 'The Loneliness Of Noam Chomsky'.[67] First she affirms that if she were asked to choose one of Noam Chomsky's major contributions to the world, it would be the fact that he has unmasked the ugly, manipulative, ruthless universe that exists behind that beautiful, sunny word 'freedom'. He has done this rationally and empirically. The mass of evidence he has marshalled to construct his case is formidable. Terrifying, actually. The starting premise of Chomsky's method is not ideological, but it is intensely political. He embarks on his course of inquiry with an anarchist's instinctive mistrust of power. He takes us on a tour through the bog of the US establishment, and leads us through the dizzying maze of corridors that connects the government, big business, and the business of managing public opinion.[68]

She then quotes the 'total isolation' Chomsky felt when contemplating, as a sixteen-year-old, the dropping of the atom bomb on Hiroshima, and concludes: 'That isolation produced one of the greatest, most radical public thinkers of our time. When the sun sets on the American empire, as it will, as it must, Noam Chomsky's work will survive.'[69] This is a fitting tribute.

It remains to examine what Chomsky has written in arguably his most important political book so far, *Hegemony or Survival: America's Quest for Global Dominance* (2003), in which he lays bare the circumstances that Roy alludes to above. For an opener Chomsky asks if the human species is likely to outsmart itself in its drive for hegemony: will it win the game of global dominance for a brief moment in time and then self-destruct, or should we be content to be 'stupid' and survive on a par with 'beetles and bacteria', species that are more successful than the human one. The prospects seem to indicate the former scenario. Chomsky can list an endless litany of events, policies and plans that set us on the way to Armageddon. The erstwhile aim of achieving US hegemony, however, can only be accomplished if the ordinary people – the masses, the punters, the workers – are kept out of it. This is the role of all governments, writes Chomsky, and 'it is far more important in the more free societies, where obedience cannot be maintained by the lash'.[70] As we shall examine in more detail in the next chapter, this is achieved through subtle propaganda and self-censorship by the makers of public opinion, the mass media. Chomsky then dissects the 'imperial grand strategy' of the US economic and political elites. In fact, the very notion of an imperial strategy is that it can change its strategy whenever it likes. When no WMDs were found in Iraq after the invasion, the US administration simply amended the strategy to attacking anyone who had the intent and ability to develop WMDs. 'Hence', Chomsky puts it bluntly, 'the refined version of the grand strategy effectively grants Washington the right of arbitrary aggression.'[71] The rule of law, internationally and domestically, must also be amended as the need arises. Treaties and UN conventions ratified by the US count for nothing. All of it must be explained by 'noble intent' on the part of the US and her fight for freedom – and anyone not with us is against us. Such rhetoric for public consumption is indistinguishable from that of common tyrants who also act on behalf of noble ideals, as did Hitler, as did Hussein. That the war on terror and every other little intervention and invasion (Chomsky reminds us again of East Timor and Kosovo) are morally good and just, as long as they are prosecuted by the 'enlightened' states of the free West, is not contestable. Chomsky quotes Tony Blair's adviser Robert Cooper, who said that 'the need for colonization is as great as ever',[72] for the sake of savages who will in time accept with gratitude the benefits of Western rule of law. We are sliding into a neo-feudalist world order whereby the imperialist United States delegates tasks to the 'alliance of the willing', while isolating itself from all outside influences. Should any of the client states create trouble, then 'regime change' must be instituted. This includes the traditional friends of the US. Chomsky puts Iraq under the spotlight and comes to the conclusion that the Bush administration will take Iraq as a test case to see if it can impose its will in the face of the most bizarre situation played out in Iraq itself. Ready to risk sacrificing thousands of troops, 'the Bush administration openly declared its intention . . . to control the world by force'.[73] Not that world domination, once achieved, is an end in itself. As with many empires before, there is the constant battle to intensify the profit margins by monopolizing business and trade. The much vaunted 'free market' becomes anything but 'free', and corporate oligarchies fight it out amongst themselves, leaving large-scale destruction in their wake. Chomsky demonstrates this in his chapter on 'dilemmas of dominance'. The tri-polar order of trading blocs – US, Europe and Asia – are forever shifting in their cunning and often use crude strategies to gain an economic advantage. Trade wars erupt between the US and Europe over subsidies. China–US relations swing between enthusiastic trade and accusations of unfair advantages – not to mention the perennial charges of theft of intellectual property. The danger of capitalist wars is on the increase again: the problems are not restricted to successful defiance in the Third World, a major theme of the Cold War years, but reach the industrial heartlands themselves.[74]

A major theme, as ever, is the 'cauldron of animosities' in the Middle East. Israel is armed to the teeth with WMDs. Should Israel ever lose control over its neighbours – far and wide – then the ultimate weapons may well be deployed, and with the full sanction of the US: 'As the official ratio of Palestinians to Israelis killed moved from twenty-to-one to close to three-to-one, attitudes in the US changed from inattention to atrocities or support for them to extreme outrage: at the atrocities directed at innocent US clients.'[75]

Since the Bush administration successfully sidelined Arafat, if not contributed to his demise, US Secretary of State Condoleezza Rice has made intensive efforts to bring democracy to Palestine compliant with US foreign policy. Premier Sharon's 'gift' to the Palestinians – the selective withdrawal from Gaza – must rate as one of the more cynical attempts to placate any vestiges of popular support for peace in the Middle East.

Chomsky then turns his attention to the 'war against terror', the aftermath of 9/11. In the first instance, any US or British government-accepted definition of 'terror' would rebound on the respective governments and make them liable for the same crimes. Both governments have succeeded in obliterating such crazy ideas from public discourse. Chomsky thus engages in the painful mathematics of terror, setting the 3,000 victims of 9/11 against the tens of thousands of documented victims that are directly attributable to acts of terror perpetrated by US forces. This has outraged the American right wing (as well as many liberals) like nothing else from Chomsky in recent times. Nothing pleases such people more so than when so-called intellectuals from client states chime in. One such example is the Australian academic and publisher Keith Windshuttle, author of 'The Hypocrisy of Noam Chomsky' in the magazine *The New Criterion*:

> Chomsky was the most conspicuous American intellectual to rationalize the Al Qaeda terrorist attacks on New York and Washington. The death toll, he argued, was minor compared to the list of Third World victims of the 'far more extreme terrorism' of United States foreign policy. Despite its calculated affront to mainstream opinion, this sentiment went down very well with Chomsky's own constituency. He has never been more popular among the academic and intellectual left than he is today . . . Chomsky's hypocrisy stands as the most revealing measure of the sorry depths to which the left-wing political activism he has done so much to propagate has now sunk.[76]

Such emotive attacks on Chomsky are ten a penny. And many of the authors are well versed in what Chomsky calls 'the art of "disappearing" unwanted facts'. What emerges is the main cause of terrorism as we know it: it is the US imposing standards that she herself does not abide by. Such hypocrisy stirs extreme antagonism in people with a sense of justice, and those at the receiving end do sometimes resort to counter-terrorism.

In the last chapter of *Hegemony or Survival* Chomsky returns to the question posed in the introduction. Given the stark scenario he has outlined in painstaking detail, is there any hope? Is it, as he puts it 'a passing nightmare'? To drive home the 'nightmare' scenario he adds the real potential of a nuclear conflagration, a fact that has also been written out of the conscience and consciousness of public opinion. Some 40,000 nuclear weapons in the former Soviet Union alone are lurking in deteriorating power centres, while US propaganda focuses its sights on the negligible nuclear threat from Iran and North Korea. Reagan's 'Star Wars' pro-gramme is enthusiastically continued by Bush and Rumsfeld, increasing the danger of an accidental trigger every day. The Cold War axiom of MAD (Mutual Assured Destruction) has gone out of the window and the Pentagon is busy modelling pre-emptive nuclear strikes. Will the US resort to such measures? Kennedy came close to it during the Cuba crisis. Bush may not have any such lin-gering scruples. American corporate power may demand no less: after all the same supreme power has demanded that the US will not accede to the Kyoto Protocol, a remedy that might save the earth from MAD by pollution from SUVs alone. The Bush adminis-tration continues to oblige. What should we do?

Chomsky has never answered this question for others. He has, however, answered the question for himself, and he is asking us to make up our minds. Now that we know the facts of the matter we must draw a personal conclusion. To act or not to act. If we decide to act, and act in unison with the masses of people who have reached a similar conclusion, then there is no telling what good things could happen. Here Chomsky is the eternal optimist, proclaiming that 'it would be a great error to conclude that the prospects are uniformly

Chomsky in India, 2001.

bleak'.[77] He lists advances in the development of a human rights culture, in the US and elsewhere. He speaks highly of solidarity movements in the Third World. He endorses the global justice movements as expressed in the World Social Forum (WSF). He mentions the very phrase that Arundhati Roy used to open the WSF in Mumbai, namely that 'another world is possible'. The choices are ours but there are only two (ever faithful to his biological principle of binary features):

> One can discern two trajectories in current history: one aiming toward hegemony, acting rationally within a lunatic doctrinal framework as it threatens survival; the other dedicated to the belief that 'another world is possible' . . . challenging the reigning ideological system and seeking to create constructive alternatives of thought, action, and institutions . . . what matters is whether we can awaken ourselves from the nightmare before it

becomes all-consuming, and bring a measure of peace and justice and hope to the world that is, right now, within the reach of our opportunity and our will.[78]

Since the publication of *Hegemony or Survival?* in 2003 there have been many other appeals by Chomsky in the same vein. As a tireless campaigner he is not averse to repeating his message again and again. In 2001 he delivered the Lakdawala Memorial Lecture in India. In 2004 and the beginning of 2005 he gave talks in Florence, Thessalonica, Athens, Hungary, London, Oxford, Manchester, Liverpool, Oldenburg, Edinburgh, Berlin, Leipzig, Ljubljana, Novigrad and Bologna – not to mention his frequent engagements in North America. He attended both World Social Forums in Brazil in 2002 and 2003. He was in Istanbul in 2002 supporting a publisher. He also travelled to the Kurdish regions of Turkey and spoke on behalf of the oppressed Kurds. In 2003 he went to Cuba at the invitation of the chair of the Latin American Association of Social Scientists (CLASCO). Back home he denounces the US embargo of Cuba.

In *Chomsky: Ideas and Ideals* (1999), Neil Smith lists a staggering 46 countries on which Chomsky has written in depth in terms of US foreign policy and/or internal conflicts. Since 1999 we can add Turkey, Pakistan, Afghanistan and many of the post-Soviet states that suffer from perennial conflict. Since 9/11 we can add a whole global dimension.

4

Reading the Newspapers

Many a talk given by Chomsky on politics and current affairs begins
with a quotation from the day's morning newspapers, often confirming the argument he is about to outline. It's an early breakfast
routine, reading four or five different daily newspapers. When at
home it's the ones he subscribes to: *Boston Globe, New York Times,
Wall Street Journal, Financial Times* and *Christian Science Monitor*. He
also has a subscription to the *Washington Post Weekly*. When abroad
it's usually a selection of the left-of-centre dailies, as the case may
has be. Chomsky has been reading newspapers for as long as he can
remember. They featured in his life from an early age – working at
the kiosk his uncle ran on Seventy-Second Street in New York:

> The newsstand itself was a very lively, intellectual center – pro-
> fessors of this and that arguing all night. And working at the
> newsstand was a lot of fun . . . the newspapers were kind of
> like an artefact. So, for example, I went for years thinking that
> there's a newspaper called Newsinmira. And the reason is, as
> people came out of the subway station and raced passed the
> newsstand, they would say 'Newsinmira,' what I heard that way,
> and I gave them two tabloids, which I later discovered were the
> *News* and the *Mirror*. And I noticed that as soon as they picked
> up the 'Newsinmira,' the first thing they opened to was the
> sports page. So this is an eight-year-old picture of the world.
> There were newspapers there, but that wasn't all there was –

that was kind of like the background of the discussions that were going on.[1]

Something that young Noam soon learned was that there were the *News* and *Mirror* type of tabloids that everybody bought – if only for the sports sections – and that there were all these alternative media in the style of pamphlets, news sheets, journals, magazines that practically nobody bought. Why was that? He would have found out when he also visited the offices of the *Freie Arbeiter Stimme* (Fraye Arbeter Shtime/ Free Voice of Labour), a weekly Jewish anarchist-orientated paper at 45 West 17th Street. Staffed by volunteers, it was operated on a shoe-string budget. The only income came from selling copies of the weekly – which few people bought. They obviously didn't get any advertising revenue from big or small business – well, they weren't exactly in favour of private property. They disseminated information for the sake of information. It was a labour of love. The tabloid news, on the other hand, were big business. If young Chomsky had had the opportunity to visit the headquarters of William Randolph Hearst's newspaper empire he would have been able to make the comparison without having to read about it in the *Freie Arbeiter Stimme*. In addition, just by standing for a time on a street corner in New York, he would have seen glimpses of that other American Dream – the super rich, the famous, the powerful – as gloated over in the society pages of the tabloid press. Read all about it! Citizen Kane! Income from the sale of copies is peanuts. Income from advertising is hugely profitable. News is secondary, if even that. Still, the tabloids shape public opinion, and that is something to think about. Chomsky thought about it a lot. His much older radical friends derided anyone who read, let alone bought, a copy of the daily tabloid press. How about studying the enemy instead of ignoring him? Not that the young Chomsky would say so at that time, but eventually he became an expert media analyst who dissected the American media industry like no other before him. This is the story of how he got there.

One important skill he acquired early on was learned from his father, who as a Jewish scholar valued text not only for its own sake, but as a means to instigate a kind of internal dialogue, talking back to the text, as it were. This tradition gives rise to the fine art of textual interpretation, annotation and the systematic archiving of any such secondary text. Excellent mental organization is called for, especially as Chomsky's filing system to this day consists of random piles of papers stacked all over the place. At least by the time Chomsky became seriously interested in linguistics he could draw on these skills and thus assemble a vast amount of notes that turned into articles and books with amazing speed. When it comes to reading newspapers every day, many people absorb a vast amount of information, often quite randomly and unrelated, and by the next day most of it is forgotten. Occasionally one strains to remember where one read such and such, for it would be good to have that information at hand now. There are those on the other

Chomsky in his new office with a poster of Bertrand Russell.

hand who are like collectors of 'useful' junk, just in case it will come in handy one day. Whenever they read an interesting article they cut it out and file it away. It may come in handy. Chomsky developed this, too, into a fine art. Look at any of his popular books on politics and current affairs and you will see a plethora of notes that direct the reader to articles that appeared in any number of newspapers. A casual count of the notes in his book *Hegemony or Survival* yields a total of 456 notes, some 212 of which refer to newspapers or news magazines.[2] Newspapers and news magazines quoted include the *New York Times, Christian Science Monitor, Los Angeles Times, Washington Post, Financial Times, Wall Street Journal, Boston Globe, Guardian, Newsweek, Observer, Independent, Irish Times, Economist, Al-Ahram Weekly, Ha'aretz, Jerusalem Post* and *Newsday*. Nobody can accuse Chomsky of citing only obscure sources!

'All the news that's fit to print' is the motto of the *New York Times* – a fitting tribute to all the news media, as it unashamedly asserts the editorial policy of someone deciding what is – and what is not – 'fit' to print. Even when a news item has been deemed 'fit' to be printed, there is a wide range of perspectives as to how such an item gets reported. Every newspaper has a political slant – the alternative press included. It is a moot point whether newspapers write for a certain readership or whether they create one, but the effect is the same. When the *Daily Mail* was launched in England in 1896 the Marquess of Salisbury termed the symbiotic relationship as 'written by office boys for office boys'.[3] Chomsky knew all that when he was a boy too. What he also learned was that the media is not only a benign 'fourth estate' that keeps governments and the business community honest, but that it can have very sinister dimensions, especially when the media becomes a tool of propaganda.

He would have learned that from many sources on his reading list, but George Orwell in particular would have confirmed his suspicions. Orwell's powerful metaphor of 'newspeak', whereby

Steven Fischer, Wolfgang Sperlich and Carol and Noam Chomsky in
New Zealand, 1998.

language itself becomes subservient to propaganda, can be applied
to many a news article ever since. Orwell, whose early work Chomsky
much admires, was essentially a reporter who chronicled what he
read and what he saw, commenting with devastating honesty and
wit on the discrepancies between the two. Quite naturally Chomsky
came to adopt Orwell's style, even if Chomsky initially grappled
more with the discrepancies between what he read in mainstream
press reports and anarcho-syndicalist pamphlets.

As Chomsky, following Orwell, began to travel the world and
actually saw many of the things that do or don't get reported in the
daily 'foreign' news, his perspective became broader and he could
comment – as did Orwell – on the discrepancies between what he
had seen and experienced (and/or researched) and what was being
reported back home. And as Barsky has put it perceptively, 'the
measurement of the distance between the realities presented by
these two sources, and the evaluation of why such a gap exists,
remained a passion for Chomsky'.[4] The operative word here is

'measurement'. Here Orwell and Chomsky diverge. Chomsky applies his scientific mind to the task of 'measuring' the discrepancies, resulting not in any great literary effort, but in exceptionally well researched treatises on the role of the mass media. Even so Chomsky's language is not obscured by scientific jargon – indeed he is twice winner of the Orwell Award, granted by the National Council of Teachers of English for 'Distinguished Contributions to Honesty and Clarity in Public Language'. It is a fitting award, in view of some criticism that his language is often dense and difficult to follow.

The actual effort in making detailed media 'measurements' might never have happened without the meeting of minds, namely the notable collaboration between Edward S. Herman and Chomsky. They came into contact with one another during the late 1960s, when Herman was a lecturer in finance at the Wharton School, University of Pennsylvania, but with a passion for media analysis, especially as related to the Vietnam War which was raging at the time. They corresponded on these matters, exchanging ideas and articles they had written or were about to write, and before long they developed a synergy that led to the idea to write something together. The first such effort ready for publication was *Counter-Revolutionary Violence* (1973). As detailed in the previous chapter it was taken out of circulation, after it was printed, by the parent company of the publisher, namely Warner Communications. Not an auspicious beginning for a pair of media analysts! A French translation appeared in 1974, but this was not exactly to the liking of the authors either. Chomsky says that 'it was mistranslated to satisfy the ideological needs of the French left at that time'.[5] Chomsky and Herman kept working on the original version and a much expanded version appeared only in 1979 as part of the two-volume set of *The Political Economy of Human Rights*. Indeed Herman later cautioned an Internet website that wanted to post the original *Counter-Revolutionary Violence* as follows:

I presume you understand that Chomsky and I greatly expanded and improved *Counterrevolutionary Violence* in the two volume set we put out in 1979 under the general heading of the *Political Economy of Human Rights*. In the first volume, *The Washington Connection and Third World Fascism*, we had a Prefatory Note that describes the suppression of CRV. If you want to put CRV onto the Web, it is important that you add a prefatory note pointing out that CRV was greatly expanded and improved in a two volume set, the first volume, [title], the second volume *After the Cataclysm: Postwar Indochina and the Reconstruction of Imperial Ideology*, both still available from South End Press.[6]

Despite the difficult gestation of their first effort, Herman and Chomsky persevered and continued their work together, culminating in *Manufacturing Consent: The Political Economy of the Mass Media* (1988). A classic in its own right, *Manufacturing Consent* became a byword for a generation or more of media watchers. The authors

Cover of Herman and Chomsky's *Manufacturing Consent.*

begin by pointing out that their idea of a 'propaganda model' as applied to the US mass media is nothing new; indeed the very term 'manufacturing consent' was coined by Walter Lippmann, an influential American columnist writing in the 1920s. What is new is the way in which the present analysis is undertaken. Herman as the economics and finance expert shines through when they announce that their analysis is a 'free market analysis with the results largely an outcome of the workings of the market forces'.[7] It just turns out that the 'free market' isn't so free after all. It is in fact very much a 'guided market system', with mostly voluntary self-censorship in the first instance.

Perhaps one should pause here and explain the use of the term 'free market', as it is usually akin to the red rag dangled by the capitalist matador before the enraged bull of Socialism. The consolidated Left sneers at the author of the famous phrase of the 'invisible hand' of the free and capitalist market fixing all there is to fix – Adam Smith. Surprisingly perhaps, Chomsky has defended Adam Smith, and his seminal book *Wealth of Nations* (1776), by noting that Smith has said no such thing. Indeed what Smith did say was that the effort of the individual worker contributes to the common good more than any effort directed from above:

> Every individual necessarily labours to render the annual revenue of the society as great as he can. He generally neither intends to promote the public interest, nor knows how much he is promoting it . . . By preferring the support of domestic to that of foreign industry, he intends only his own security; and by directing that industry in such a manner as its produce may be of the greatest value, he intends only his own gain, and he is in this, as in many other cases, led by an invisible hand to promote an end which was no part of his intention. Nor is it always the worse for society that it was no part of his intention. By pursuing his own interest he frequently promotes that of the society more effectually than

when he really intends to promote it. I have never known much good done by those who affected to trade for the public good.[8]

Smith, according to Chomsky, was thus much misunderstood in his arguments for a 'free market'. Capitalism as we have it today is anything but 'free'. Indeed Smith – however absurd it may sound – is not too far away from the ideas of anarcho-syndicalism in his call for individual freedom to engage in trade and commerce without the interference of any governmental or corporate superstructure (designed to stifle, control and suppress such freedoms, as the case may be). Chomsky refers to Rocker, who argued that classical liberalism (as espoused by Smith and others) was destroyed on the rock of capitalism, and that the anarchist tradition is its natural successor.

In any case, the metaphor of a 'free market' – where 'free' has the socialist libertarian meaning – can be transferred to a 'free media', as Herman and Chomsky do. The big question then is, why are the media not free? Why, at its worst, are the media merely a tool of crude propaganda? The answers to these questions, proffered by Herman and Chomsky, have now become widely accepted in radical media critiques – if not occasionally reaching even into mainstream critiques. The Herman and Chomsky 'propaganda model' posits four filters of control, detailed as follows:

1. Size, ownership, and profit orientation of the mass media
2. The advertising licence to do business
3. Sourcing mass-media news
4. Flak and the enforcer

Beginning with 'Filter No. 1', one may note that in theory anyone can start a newspaper, be it the *Freie Arbeiter Stimme* or the *New York Times*. That the former has a minute distribution compared to the latter is at the heart of the matter. The *Freie Arbeiter Stimme* simply doesn't have the financial means to boost its circulation; in other words the *Freie Arbeiter Stimme* operates at the pre-industrial level while the *New York Times* is a fine example of having achieved a high level of the 'industrialization of the press'.[9] The very idea of the 'mass media' is intimately connected to 'mass production', whereby enormous resources are required to get going in the first place. Capital and human resource investment is of such a magnitude that only the big players in the market can pull it off. Herman and Chomsky provide data for start-up costs for a New York City newspaper in 1851 to be in the vicinity of $69,000, rising to between 6 and 18 million dollars in the 1920s. No data is available for estimated start-up costs today, but the figures are said to be in the billions. When media mogul Rupert Murdoch shifted production facilities in London in the mid-1980s, he not only defeated the printers' unions but also introduced highly automated processes that dispensed with labour costs and thus increased his profit margins a thousand-fold. Print, radio and television became corporate conglomerates that raked in huge profits. Murdoch, as a prime example, extended his tentacles all over the world, creating one of the largest global corporations ever seen. No wonder the poor old *Freie Arbeiter Stimme* folded in 1977 while the *New York Times* becomes ever more profitable. Selling the news is thus no different from flogging cars and shampoo. It is painfully obvious that those owning and running the mass media couldn't care less about anything as long as it sells, and sells well. To maintain a most favourable business climate with plenty of tax breaks and anti-union legislation there is a cosy symbiosis with the governments of the day, doing each other favours like no others. As Herman and Chomsky put it with a touch of irony, 'the political ties of the media have been impressive'.[10]

Filter no. 2 is in place for those that made it through Filter no. 1. Having somehow convinced our libertarian bankers that they should inject a few billion dollars into our new mass media syndicate, here comes the second obstacle – or saviour, as the case may be. The industrial age and mass production have come up with another amazing advance, namely to sell vast amounts of goods that nobody needs but everyone wants. The trick was to turn the consumer into Pavlov's dog – through the use of advertising. The so-called science of behaviourism – the one Chomsky fought so hard against in linguistics and philosophy – has reached new heights in creating consumer demand even before the supply is ready to hit the shelves. The happy (and necessary) union of advertising and the mass media changed our world into the out and out consumer society we are now. There is now one, and only one, *raison d'être* for the ever increasing media circulation and exposure: enabling advertisers to reach larger and larger numbers of consumers, thus increasing sales for their clients, thus increasing profits for the corporations involved. We need 'the advertising licence to do business' that is Filter no. 2.

In taking our hypothetical mass-media newspaper to the next level we must squeeze through Filter no. 3. In between the advertising copy we need some actual news items to fill up the space, and provide some pretence for calling it a newspaper. We could just employ a few clever journalists to make it all up, but as that's already being done quite successfully we must find another market niche. To send out our correspondents to the four corners of the world would be hugely expensive unless we could sell their news to all the other newspapers as well – but that's also being done already by new agencies such as Reuters and AP. Yet there is more, much more. Herman and Chomsky demonstrate through many examples that a lot of the news is also pre-written by the US government and by the publicity machines of the corporations. The infamous government and corporate 'press releases' are only the tip of an iceberg. Every corporate and governmental structure these days includes a publicity department charged to put a positive spin on everything that happens. Those most adept at turning bad news into good news get the honorary title 'spin doctor'. Finally, as Herman and Chomsky point out, this is the age of the 'expert' and every news item, especially when presented on radio and television, needs 'expert analysis' lest the audience make up their own minds as to what it all means. The news is thus a fully packaged industrial product, marketed and sold like fast food. The consumer of news only has to swallow what has been fully pre-digested for him and her. At least, now that Herman and Chomsky have told us all about it, it is possible to put a positive spin on such bad news, since we can now read between the lines and extract the real news by default. After all, some propaganda and 'infotainment' is so dumb it doesn't need much effort to see through it. What remains the biggest problem for our 'free' media is how to source and how to report all the news that in the first instance was not deemed fit to print by the corporate media.

Should anyone be game enough – as the occasional idealistic journalist might be – to report on crimes committed by the US government, then Filter no. 4 sets in. Herman and Chomsky's military metaphors of 'flak and the enforcers' are most apt for totalitarian states where inconvenient journalists are simply exiled, jailed or shot. In an open representative democracy, such as the US, more subtle methods must be applied. Even when internecine warfare breaks out among the political establishment, for example during the Watergate scandal, the media must be seen to be 'fair' at all times. It was only when the FBI leaked the news of Nixon's crimes that the press was allowed to engage in a heroic act of 'investigative journalism' and spill the beans. Endless pontificating has followed the farcical revelation in 2005 of the identity of the FBI 'deep throat'; here is an example from the *Washington Post*:

> The Watergate investigation brought fame to *The Washington Post* and the reporting team of Bob Woodward and Carl Bernstein. The duo unraveled a web of political spying and sabotage that had all the elements of a Hollywood saga. In the end, after 40 government officials were indicted and a president resigned, many would conclude that the system of checks and balances

worked. Yet, the triangular relationship between public officials, the media and the public was altered forever.[11]

In relation to Watergate, Herman and Chomsky mention in passing in *Manufacturing Consent* that a far greater scandal at the time never received any mass-media coverage, namely that of the COINTELPRO, the FBI-led counter-activist programme discussed in chapter Three. Watergate was a tea party compared with the government crimes exposed in the courts when COINTELPRO was discovered. What was the difference? Watergate was a trivial annoyance to the very rich and powerful, while COINTELPRO was just doing things like murdering black organizers, illegally destroying small left journals, undermining the women's movement, and so on. That tells us more about Watergate than the sum total that has been written about it in more than thirty years.

Hence, despite the penchant of the mass media for using hyperbole ('the world was changed forever'), very little truly investigative journalism has in fact been allowed to be published in the US. Herman and Chomsky note various media watchdog organizations, such as Accuracy in Media (AIM), whose function is 'to harass the media and put pressure on them to follow the corporate agenda and a hard-line, right-wing foreign policy'.[12] An example is provided by AIM's reaction to statements from the 'liberal media', such as the *Washington Post*:

Now that a stroke victim with dementia has been trotted forward as Deep Throat, the liberal media have been patting themselves on the back for bringing down President Richard Nixon. But as one of our readers, Creag Banta, noted, 'As long as reporting on Watergate ends with Nixon's resignation and does not include boat people and killing fields, the true fear driving Nixon's actions, the story is incomplete and inaccurate.'[13]

This is a scarcely veiled warning to journalists to leave the incumbent president, George W. Bush, alone, even if he were to be implicated in crimes so horrendous that even the FBI couldn't keep quiet about them. See what happens to supergrasses: they have 'strokes' and suffer from 'dementia'. Thus 'the producers of flak reinforce the command of political authority in its news-management activities'.[14]

Given that our really 'free' media cannot even trickle through one filter, let alone through four, the chances of our *Freie Arbeiter Stimme* being relaunched as a daily with mass circulation are absolutely nil.

Manufacturing Consent goes on to detail other propaganda tools before it concentrates on concrete examples of what gets reported and what not, the real crux of the matter. In the chapter entitled 'Worthy and Unworthy Victims' there is a statistical analysis of news reports about a murdered Polish priest (October 1984) versus some one hundred religious murder victims in Latin America. The *New York Times* yields a 100:51 ratio of column inches in favour of the Polish priest (coverage is for an eighteen-month period). In some ten tables and three extensive appendices there is a wealth of data, and the reader can make up his/her mind about the implications. Another example of 'worthy' versus 'unworthy' victims concerns the Khmer Rouge in Cambodia: when they terrorized the Cambodian population they were vilified in the American media (justly so), but when they later resisted the liberation of Cambodia itself via the Vietnamese, the scenario reversed in a perverse way, with the Khmer Rouge becoming freedom fighters and the Vietnamese the oppressors. According to Herman and Chomsky: 'After early efforts to charge the Vietnamese with "genocide", the condemnation of the official enemy shifted to the terrible acts of "the Prussians of Asia", who have "subjugated and impoverished" Cambodia since overthrowing Pol Pot, according to the editors of the *New York Times*.'[15]

It is of course not only the *New York Times* that is implicated, for Herman and Chomsky detail many other American media empires who conspire to 'manufacture consent'. The exercise of comparing death and destruction on one side with death and destruction on the other has irritated many detractors, saying that it belittles death and destruction on both sides. However, this is clearly not the purpose of the book. It is rather the absolute claim that death and destruction is so abhorrent that all such acts must be reported with equal disdain and distaste. It is an absolute betrayal of human value when one death is vilified and the other is justified, or, in media terms, one death is news, the other is not. It comes down to a new barbarism that says evil people deserve to die without mention but the murder of a single good person is worthy of news. Since we know who the arbiters of good and evil are, we rest our case, as did George Orwell in *Nineteen Eighty-four*.

Manufacturing Consent contains a mass of detail, meticulously researched and referenced. Some readers find the relentless onslaught of quotations and citations unsettling. Haven't Herman and Chomsky already made their point?, one may ask. Well, this is a prime example of the scientific method – it's not about scoring points but about presenting the indisputable facts of the matter: the reader can make up his or her mind accordingly. The book remains a bestseller among the Chomsky titles; its continuing topicality is indicated by *Filtering the News: Essays on Herman and Chomsky's Propaganda Model*, edited by Jeffery Klaehn and published in 2005 by another alternative-cum-anarchist media outlet, appropriately named Black Rose Books.

Given the apparent popularity of such media critiques, one does wonder, though, how the *New York Times* and all the other malefactors implicated in *Manufacturing Consent*, haven't yet gone out of business. Is it the case that the many have heard about the book but only a few have actually read it? As mentioned before, the book was followed by a documentary of the same name; since the latter has achieved a certain cult status on the alternative film circuits, there has been much confusion as to what it all means. Since this is a media issue in itself, it is worth turning things around and looking at this phenomenon from the very perspective that Herman and Chomsky have given us.

In the first instance, Chomsky has not been very 'media savvy' when it comes to his own public appearances, not minding if people record his speeches on audio and video, or worrying who holds the copyrights to his interviews. It was only as he reached a sort of celebrity status, with people following him wherever he went and recording it all for posterity, that he accepted some advice and half-heartedly employed a sort of media consultant to look after things like copyright and royalties. When two Canadian filmmakers, Mark Achbar and Peter Wintonick, approached him in the early 1990s with their project to shoot the film *Manufacturing Consent*, Chomsky said, sure, go ahead, and do whatever you have to do. After all, these guys weren't in it for the money. It wasn't Hollywood. Not that Chomsky took an active interest in the proceedings. Anyway, he had been on television before, in North America, Europe, on the BBC and even on Dutch television with Foucault. So Achbar and Wintonick shot new footage and used old material, mainly of Chomsky talking and giving speeches. Available news footage relating to topics such as Indonesia and East Timor were also used. The finished product, *Manufacturing Consent: Noam Chomsky and the Media*, was first screened in 1992 and an entry in Wikipedia (the free on-line encyclopaedia) informs us that until 2003 'it was the most successful documentary in Canadian history, playing theatrically in over 300 cities around the world; winning 22 awards; appearing in more than 50 international film festivals; and being broadcast in over 30 markets. It has also been translated into a dozen languages.'[16]

Incredibly perhaps, Chomsky has claimed that he has never seen the film and is unlikely to do so. Reason? 'I hate watching or hearing myself.'[17] I can perhaps understand the stance, having had such an experience myself. But then again, nobody bothered to repeat the experience so that I might eventually get accustomed to it. Surely Chomsky must have had the odd peek himself, since by 2005 his filmography lists a staggering 28 titles in which he appears?[18] Alas, he admits to only one, when he was asked to lead a discussion section while Mark Achbar's documentary *The Corporation* was shown in a small Cambridge theatre – and saw himself on the screen.

It is probably safe to say that many of his screen appearances are less than exciting, and not worth watching if you've read the book or heard the talk in person (or listened to the audio tape). The latest offering is a case in point: the 2005 DVD version of *Noam Chomsky: Rebel without a Pause* (originally a Canadian television production released in 2003). A film crew (surely shooting on a shoestring budget, judging by the quality of the footage) follows Chomsky around for a week on a public lecturing and speaking tour at a university in Canada. Interspersed with a few short interviews with others, including Carol Chomsky, the rest is all of Chomsky speaking, from the lectern and in discussion groups. The visuals are rather boring. If I were Chomsky I wouldn't watch it either. It's like watching oneself in the mirror for 60 minutes or so. Perhaps he should withdraw permission for it to be screened in public. It is most definitely a media matter because Chomsky is fast becoming a media commodity, to be released onto a sizeable market of left-of-centre consumers who watch the movie but never read the book. Still, it's only a storm in a teacup when compared to the real media issues contained in the real *Manufacturing Consent*.

Book and film made Chomsky's name like nothing else before – and possibly since. It seems a bit unfair on Herman, who wrote, after all, most of the book. Yet he and Chomsky remain close: in 2003, for example, he defended his co-author against a slanderous article, 'My Very, Very Allergic Reaction to Noam Chomsky: Khmer Rouge, Faurisson, Milosevic', written by Brad Delong ,a neo-liberal economist. Herman's rebuttal was aptly titled: 'My Very, Very Allergic Reaction to Brad Delong on Chomsky'.[19]

Given that Herman and Chomsky had established a very plausible 'propaganda model', it seemed inevitable that Chomsky would

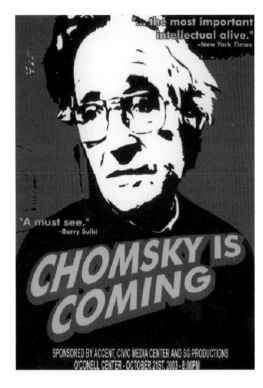

"...the most important intellectual alive."
-New York Times

"A must see."
-Barry Suikl

CHOMSKY IS COMING

SPONSORED BY ACCENT, CIVIC MEDIA CENTER AND SG PRODUCTIONS
O'CONELL CENTER - OCTOBER 21ST, 2003 - 8:00PM

The poster for Chomsky's talk given at the University of Florida, 2003.

have to follow up and comment on world events as time passes, stripping away the layers of propaganda, telling us what the real news is and what not. He does not disappoint. Since *Manufacturing Consent* there have been many talks, articles and books dealing specifically with mass-media issues – far too numerous to list here. Only one year after the publication of *Manufacturing Consent*, Chomsky published *Necessary Illusions: Thought Control in Democratic Societies*. Once more, it is uncompromising in its denunciation of all that is wrong with the US and like-minded democracies:

> I will be primarily concerned with one aspect: thought control, as conducted through the agency of the national media and

related elements of the elite intellectual culture. There is, in my opinion, much too little inquiry into these matters. My personal feeling is that citizens of the democratic societies should undertake a course of intellectual self-defense to protect themselves from manipulation and control, and to lay the basis for more meaningful democracy. It is this concern that motivates the material that follows, and much of the work cited in the course of the discussion.[20]

Much wider in scope than *Manufacturing Consent*, this book nevertheless has its main focus on the American media, particularly in the first chapter, which is entitled 'Democracy and the Media'. Again supported by voluminous footnotes and appendices, there is an emphasis on the data that in turn leads to inescapable conclusions, harsh as they may be. Furthermore there is the strong historical aspect that points to previous studies and points of view, so that the reader may see the evolution of particular developments and be in a better position to react to deep-rooted social phenomena. Chomsky's views on democracy are particularly revealing, inasmuch as they are a devastating critique of the status quo. Three main themes emerge:

1. Capitalist democracy of the West equals Soviet-style democracy of the East.
2. Authoritarian American democracy started with the Founding Fathers.
3. The masses are denied access to democracy run by specialist classes.

In almost biblical terms Chomsky rails against those who perpetuate the crime of withholding true democracy from ordinary people:

At its root, the logic is that of the Grand Inquisitor, who bitterly assailed Christ for offering people freedom and thus condemning them to misery. The Church must correct the evil work of Christ by offering the miserable mass of humanity the gift they most desire and need: absolute submission. It must 'vanquish freedom' so as 'to make men happy' and provide the total 'community of worship' that they avidly seek. In the modern secular age, this means worship of the state religion, which in the Western democracies incorporates the doctrine of submission to the masters of the system of public subsidy, private profit, called free enterprise. The people must be kept in ignorance, reduced to jingoist incantations, for their own good. And like the Grand Inquisitor, who employs the forces of miracle, mystery, and authority 'to conquer and hold captive for ever the conscience of these impotent rebels for their happiness' and to deny them the freedom of choice they so fear and despise, so the 'cool observers' must create the 'necessary illusions' and 'emotionally potent oversimplifications' that keep the ignorant and stupid masses disciplined and content.[21]

Note that the expression 'necessary illusions' (and the book's title) are derived from Reinhold Niebuhr (1932), an influential American intellectual commissar who espoused such views. One must be reminded that Chomsky, as an anarcho-syndicalist, is bound to be dismissive of any style of democracy that lacks full participation of the masses, organized at local level. The implications for the media, in terms of a truly democratic model, are not really addressed in either *Manufacturing Consent* or *Necessary Illusions*, unless one is able to make the jump from what the media is to what it should be. By describing the faults of any system one should be able to discern the correct system, which in terms of democracy and the media are common sense ideas for Chomsky that need no great elaboration. He does provide the occasional hint though, by lending his support to grassroots efforts to 'democratise the media' in a meaningful way:

Under the heading 'Brazilian bishops support plan to democratize media,' a church-based South American journal describes a proposal being debated in the constituent assembly that 'would open up Brazil's powerful and highly concentrated media to citizen participation.' 'Brazil's Catholic bishops are among the principal advocates [of this] . . . legislative proposal to democratize the country's communications media,' the report continues, noting that 'Brazilian TV is in the hands of five big networks [while] . . . eight huge multinational corporations and various state enterprises account for the majority of all communications advertising.' The proposal 'envisions the creation of a National Communications Council made up of civilian and government representatives [that] . . . would develop a democratic communications policy and grant licenses to radio and television operations.' 'The Brazilian Conference of Catholic Bishops has repeatedly stressed the importance of the communications media and pushed for grassroots participation. It has chosen communications as the theme of its 1989 Lenten campaign,' an annual 'parish-level campaign of reflection about some social issue' initiated by the Bishops' Conference.[22]

That such efforts are anathema in the United States is of course not surprising. Still, Chomsky is forever pointing out that all is not lost and that the odd individual in American power structures, past and present, does contribute worthwhile judgements, for example Justice Oliver Wendell Holmes in 1919, whom Chomsky lauds for saying that, in a typically unorthodox interpretation of 'free market', 'the best test of truth is the power of the thought to get itself accepted in the competition of the market' through 'free trade in ideas'.[23] At least one can attribute such optimism to the hard sciences, where the filters are least strong. But pessimism might be called for in the social and political world, where the filters of control are overwhelming.

Following on, it must be said that Chomsky's work on media issues has had a deep impact on the rise of the alternative media in the US and internationally. Today there are literally thousands of so-called alternative radio stations, Internet sites and publishers who often feature the work of Chomsky. Lydia Sargent and Michael Albert, for example, established South End Press, which has published many of Chomsky's books, including *Necessary Illusions*. Being technologically savvy, they have since spawned *z Magazine* and *z Net*, which has an incredible amount of material available online, enough to make any political activist's heart sing.[24] Another Chomsky fan in the US media world is Roger Leisner of Radio Free Maine, which describes itself as 'Voices of the Left – Unedited and Uncensored'.[25] Leisner is one of those enthusiasts who follows Chomsky with camera and microphone to record every word he utters in public: he has a selection of more than a hundred audio and video tapes, all for sale at cost price. Indeed, radio is Chomsky's favourite medium. Even in New Zealand, where virtually all the 'voices of the left' are in deep sleep, there is a small radio station called, you guessed it, Radio Chomsky.

Let us conclude, though, with yet another seminal contribution to mass-media issues. It is the second edition of *Media Control: The Spectacular Achievements of Propaganda* (2002). Typical of recent Chomsky publications, it is a compilation of the old and the new, the former of which was published in 1991 under the same title. The 'new' includes an article entitled 'The Journalist from Mars', which in turn is based on a talk given at the celebrations for the fifteenth anniversary of Fairness and Accuracy in Reporting (FAIR) in New York on 23 January 2002. As a final retort to journalists and newspaper publishers everywhere, let us check out this Martian metaphor, which has been applied by Chomsky and many others before in an effort to demonstrate how crazy these so-called humans on Planet Earth really are. Chomsky begins by asking 'how the media have handled the major story of the past months, the issue of the "war on terrorism," so-called, specifically in the Islamic world'. Then he introduces his man from Mars – gender implications included:

> Let's approach this by kind of a thought experiment. Imagine an intelligent Martian – I'm told that by convention, Martians are males, so I'll refer to it as 'he'. Suppose that this Martian went to Harvard and Columbia Journalism School and learned all kinds of high-minded things, and actually believes them. How would the Martian handle a story like this?[26]

Chomsky's Martian answers with a lengthy but extremely important history lesson, a notion often ignored by mainstream journalists who seek to sensationalize the here and now by situating it in a vacuum of unrelated events. Again Chomsky takes exception to the present catch-phrase of 'everything has changed with 9/11' by pointing out that the 'new' war on terrorism is merely a cynical continuation of us foreign policy that dates back to the 1980s, if not before:

> I think he would begin with some factual observations that he'd send back to the journal on Mars. One factual observation is that the war on terrorism was not declared on September 11; rather, it was redeclared, using the same rhetoric as the first declaration twenty years earlier. The Reagan administration, as you know, I'm sure, came into office announcing that a war on terrorism would be the core of us foreign policy, and it condemned what the president called the 'evil scourge of terrorism.' The main focus was state-supported international terrorism in the Islamic world, and at that time also in Central America. International terrorism was described as a plague spread by 'depraved opponents of civilization itself,' in 'a return to barbarism in the modern age.' Actually, I'm quoting the administration moderate, Secretary of State George Shultz. The phrase I quoted from Reagan had to do with terrorism in the Middle East, and it was

the year 1985. That was the year in which international terrorism in that region was selected by editors as the lead story of the year in an annual Associated Press poll, so point one that our Martian would report is that the year 2001 is the second time that this has been the main lead story, and that the war on terrorism has been redeclared pretty much as before. Furthermore, there's a striking continuity; the same people are in leading positions. So Donald Rumsfeld is running the military component of the second phase of the war on terrorism, and he was Reagan's special envoy to the Middle East during the first phase of the war on terrorism, including the peak year, 1985. The person who was just appointed a couple of months ago to be in charge of the diplomatic component of the war at the United Nations is John Negroponte, who during the first phase was supervising US operations in Honduras, which was the main base for the US war against terror in the first phase.[27]

Here Chomsky's political *nous* is as sharp as it has ever been. Note that since then Negroponte has moved on to take charge of Iraq (as proconsul and US ambassador to Iraq) and recently moved again to become Director of National Intelligence, a misnomer if there ever was one.

Let us close this and all other issues with Chomsky's simple but devastating truth about the matter of terrorism and how it is reported in the mass media – and according to the propaganda model: 'It's only terrorism if they do it to us. When we do much worse to them, it's not terrorism. Again, the universal principle. Well, the Martian might notice that, even if it's not discussable here.'[28]

Returning from Mars, here is the real Chomsky in his home in Lexington, poring over his newspapers at breakfast. It is a veritable paper trail – clues to the left, clues to the right. The case will never be closed until freedom is realized in the US and the rest of the world. As he says, it's up to you and me.

References

1 A Working Life

1 Noam Chomsky, *Knowledge of Language* (New York, 1986), p. xxvii; cited in James McGilvray, *Chomsky* (Cambridge, 1999), p. 239.
2 Carsten Volkery, 'Noam Chomsky, Der Grossvater der Amerika-Kritiker', *Spiegel Online*, 25 March 2005; text available online at http://www.spiegel.de/politik/deutschland/0,1518,348276,00.html (accessed 3 July 2005).
3 Public messages for Noam Chomsky's 70th birthday, posted online at http://www.zmag.org/noambirth.htm (accessed 3 July 2005).
4 Robert F. Barsky, *Noam Chomsky: A Life of Dissent* (Cambridge, MA, 1997), p. 13.
5 *Ibid.*, p. 21.
6 Noam Chomsky, *The Chomsky Reader*, ed. James Peck (New York, 1987), p. 11; also cited in Barsky, *Chomsky*, p. 23.
7 Harry Kreisler, 'Conversation with Noam Chomsky' (Berkeley, 2002); transcript available on http://www.chomsky.info/interviews/20020322.htm (accessed 1 July 2005).
8 Chomsky, *Chomsky Reader*, p. 7; also cited in Barsky, *Chomsky*, p. 47.
9 Samuel Hughes, 'The way they were (and are)', *University of Pennsylvania Gazette* (July–August 2001).
10 *Ibid.*, p. 82.
11 Carol Chomsky, *The Acquisition of Syntax in Children from Five to Ten* (Cambridge, MA, 1969).

2 Linguist and Philosopher

1 Robert F. Barsky, *Noam Chomsky: A Life of Dissent* (Cambridge, MA,

1997), p. 95.

2 Noam Chomsky, *Cartesian Linguistics* (New York, 1966).

3 David Crystal, *A Dictionary of Linguistics and Phonetics* (Oxford, 1991), pp. 258–9.

4 Ferdinand de Saussure, *Course in General Linguistics* (New York, 1959).

5 Roman Jakobson, *Selected Writings*, I: *Phonological Studies* (The Hague, 1962).

6 Claude Lévi-Strauss, *Tristes Tropiques* (New York, 1963).

7 Leonard Bloomfield, *Language* (New York, 1933).

8 B. F. Skinner, *Verbal Behavior* (New York, 1957).

9 Noam Chomsky, 'A Review of B. F. Skinner's *Verbal Behavior*', *Language*, XXXV/1 (1959), pp. 26–58.

10 See also Barsky, *Chomsky*, chapter 1.

11 Zellig S. Harris, *Methods in Structural Linguistics* (Chicago, 1951).

12 Barsky, *Chomsky*, p. 53.

13 Noam Chomsky, 'The Biolinguistic Perspective after 50 Years' (speech delivered at the University of Florence, Italy, April 2004)

14 Samuel Hughes, 'The way they were (and are)', *University of Pennsylvania Gazette* (July–August 2001).

15 Barsky, *Chomsky*, p. 86.

16 Ray C. Dougherty, *Natural Language Computing* (Hillsdale, NJ, 1994), p. viii.

17 Gilbert Harman, ed., *On Noam Chomsky: Critical Essays* (New York, 1974), p. vii.

18 Noam Chomsky, *Language and Politics* (Montreal, 1988), p. 190.

19 Bertrand Russell, *The History of Western Philosophy* (London, 1946, reprinted 1979), p. 634.

20 Donald Davidson and Jaako Hintikka, eds, *Words and Objections: Essays on the Work of W. V. Quine* (Dordrecht, 1969), p. 64.

21 Noam Chomsky, personal communication, 2005.

22 Noam Chomsky, *Aspects of the Theory of Syntax* (Cambridge, MA, 1965).

23 Chomsky, *Aspects*, pp. 128–47.

24 Available at http://www.amazon.com/exec/obidos/tg/detail/-/0060412763/qid=1120108283/sr=1- 2/ref=sr_1_2/103-0618543-1252605?v=glance&s=books (accessed 30 June 2005).

25 Crystal, *Dictionary of Linguistics*, p. 383.

26 Neil Smith, *Chomsky: Ideas and Ideals* (Cambridge, 1999).

27 *Ibid.*, p. 19.

28 Andrea Mechelli and others, 'Neurolinguistics: Structural Plasticity in the Bilingual Brain', *Nature*, 431 (2004), p. 757.

29 Smith, *Chomsky*, p. 69.

30 Noam Chomsky, *Barriers* (Cambridge, MA, 1986), p. 1.

31 Noam Chomsky, *Rules and Representations* (New York, 1980), p. 46.

32 Chomsky, *Rules*, p. 215.

33 L. S. Ramaiah and T. V. Prafulla Chandra, *Noam Chomsky: a Bibliography* (Gurgaon, 1984).

34 Randy Allen Harris, *The Linguistics Wars* (New York, 1993).

35 Smith, *Chomsky*, pp. 208–9.

36 Barsky, *Chomsky*, p. 183.

37 David Adger, *Core Syntax: a Minimalist Approach* (Oxford, 2003), p. 367.

3 Political Activist

1 Harry Kreisler, 'Conversation with Noam Chomsky' (Berkeley, 2002); transcript available on http://www.chomsky.info/interviews/20020322.htm (accessed 1 July 2005).

2 Kreisler, 'Chomsky'.

3 Rudolph Rocker, *Anarchism and Anarcho-Syndicalism* (London, 1973); earlier versions appeared in various pamphlets with unknown publication dates. A comprehensive bibliography of the works of Rudolph Rocker is available on http://flag.blackened.net/rocker/biblio.htm (accessed 1 July 2005). The text of the article cited is also available on http://flag.blackened.net/rocker/aasind.htm#struggle (accessed 1 July 2005). Another source of Rocker's work is the Anarchist Archives maintained by D. Ward on http://dwardmac.pitzer.edu/Anarchist_Archives/index.html (accessed 1 July 2005). Note that Rocker also wrote an article, 'The Tragedy of Spain', which appeared in 1937 in the *Freie Arbeiter Stimme*, the New York Jewish anarchist weekly magazine that Chomsky was in the habit of reading.

4 Roderick Kedward, *The Anarchists* (London, 1971), p. 13.

5 Rudolph Rocker, 'Anarchism and Sovietism'; text available on

http://flag.blackened.net/rocker/soviet.htm (accessed 1 July 2005).

6 Noam Chomsky, *Hegemony or Survival* (Crows Nest, NSW, 2003), p. 189.

7 Kedward, *Anarchists*, p. 14.

8 Harriet Feinberg, *Elsie Chomsky: A Life in Jewish Education* (Cambridge, MA, 1999), p. 17.

9 Neil Smith, *Chomsky: Ideas and Ideals* (Cambridge, 1999).

10 Rudolph Rocker, *Anarcho-Syndicalism: Theory and Practice. An Introduction to a Subject which the Spanish War Has Brought into Overwhelming Prominence* (London, 1938).

11 Bertrand Russell, *Roads to Freedom* (3rd edn, London, 1948), p. 6.

12 Robert F. Barsky, *Noam Chomsky: A Life of Dissent* (Cambridge, MA, 1998), p. 47.

13 Barsky, *Chomsky*, chapter 2: 'Zellig Harris, Avukah, and Hashomer Hatzair'.

14 Barsky, *Chomsky*, p. 121.

15 *Ibid*.

16 Cited from the website of RESIST at http://www.resistinc.org/resist/board.html#paullauter (accessed 1 July 2005).

17 http://www.resistinc.org/index.html (accessed 1 July 2005).

18 http://www.resistinc.org/resist/the_call.html (accessed 1 July 2005).

19 Barsky, *Chomsky*, p. 129.

20 Ron Chepesiuk, *Sixties Radicals, Then and Now* (Jefferson, NC, 1995), pp. 133–46.

21 Chomsky, personal communication.

22 Noam Chomsky, *American Power and the New Mandarins* (New York, 1969), p. 93.

23 *Ibid*., p. 297.

24 Smith, *Chomsky* (back cover).

25 Barsky, *Chomsky*, p. 138.

26 *Ibid*., p. 161.

27 The text of the original manuscript and the history of its suppression is available on http://mass-multi-media.com/CRV/ (accessed 1 July 2005).

28 Rudolph Rocker, *Anarchosyndicalism* (London, 1938), p. 31.

29 *Ibid*., p. 94.

30 Diego Abad de Santillan, *After the Revolution* (New York, 1937), p. 86.

31 Michael Bakunin, *Bakunin on Anarchy*, ed. and trans. Sam Dolgoff (New

York, 1972).

32 Noam Chomsky, 'Notes on Anarchism', in *For Reasons of State* (London, 1973); the text cited here is from the version on the 'official Chomsky web-site' at http://www.chomsky.info/books/state01.htm (accessed 1 July 2005), unpaginated.

33 Cited in Daniel Guérin, *Anarchism: From Theory to Practice*, trans. Mary Klopper (New York, 1970), no page reference given.

34 Chomsky, 'Notes on Anarchism'.

35 Karl Marx, *The Civil War in France* (New York, 1871, reprinted 1941), pp.77–8.

36 Chomsky, 'Notes on Anarchism'.

37 *Ibid.*

38 Cited on the website of the Federation of American Scientists at http://www.fas.org/irp/world/chile/allende.htm (accessed 1 July 2005).

39 A history of Nicaragua is available online at http://library.thinkquest.org/17749/mainhistory.html (accessed 1 July 2005).

40 Noam Chomsky, *On Power and Ideology: The Managua Lectures* (Boston, 1987), p. 6.

41 *Ibid.*, p. 3.

42 Noam Chomsky and Edward S. Herman, 'The Nazi Parallel: The National Security State and the Churches', in *The Washington Connection and Third World Fascism* (Boston, 1979); citation from a text version available at http://www.thirdworldtraveler.com/Herman%20/ NaziParallelFascism_Herman.html (accessed 1 July 2005), unpaginated.

43 The full text of the Concordat is available at http://www.newadvent.org/library/docs_ss33co.htm (accessed 1 July 2005).

44 Article posted online at http://www.greenleft.org.au/back/2005/621/621p19.htm (accessed 1 July 2005).

45 Chomsky, *On Power and Ideology*.

46 Noam Chomsky, 'Central America: The Next Phase', posted on *Z Magazine*, 1988, available online at http://www.zmag.org/chomsky/articles/z8803-CA-next-phase.html (accessed 1 July 2005).

47 Noam Chomsky, 'Interview', *Leviathan*, 1/1–3 (1977), pp. 6–9.

48 *Ibid.*

49 Noam Chomsky, 'Scenes from the Uprising', *z Magazine* (1988); text online at http://www.zmag.org/chomsky/articles/z8807-uprising.html (accessed 1 July 2005).

50 Noam Chomsky, 'War is Peace', in *Fateful Triangle* (Boston, 1999); text online at http://www.chomsky.info/books/fateful01.htm (accessed 1 July 2005), unpaginated.

51 Noam Chomsky, 'Interview', *Shmate: A Journal of Progressive Jewish Thought*, 20 (1988), pp. 24–32. Note that this is a very small publication and the transcript may be based on a conversation rather than a taped interview.

52 Deborah E. Lipstadt, 'Deniers, Relativists and Pseudo-Scholarship', *Dimensions*, VI/1(1991); text online at http://www.adl.org/Braun/dim_14_1_deniers_print.asp?&MSHiC=125 2&L=10&W=chomsky+CHOMSKYS+&Pre=%3CFONT+STYLE%3D%22 color%3A+%23000000%3B+background%2Dcolor%3A+%23FFFF00%22 %3E&Post=%3C%2FFONT%3E (accessed 1 July 2005).

53 Noam Chomsky, *Rogue States* (Boston, 2000), p. 51.

54 Full text available online at http://www.motherjones.com/news/special_reports/east_timor/evidence/nairn.html (accessed 1 July 2005).

55 Alex Burns, 'Operation Mindcrime: the Selling of Noam Chomsky' (2001); text online at http://www.disinfo.com/archive/pages/article/id589/pg1/ (accessed 1 July 2005).

56 *Ibid.*

57 *Ibid.*

58 Cited in Burns, 'Operation Mindcrime', p. 3.

59 *Ibid.*, p. 8.

60 Keith Locke, *Otago Daily Times* and the *Evening Post*, 23 November 1998.

61 Chomsky, *Hegemony or Survival*, p. 54.

62 East Timorese Movement Against the Occupation of the Timor Sea (19 April 2004), full text available online at http://www.etan.org/news/2004/04mkott.htm (accessed 1 July 2005).

63 Noam Chomsky, *September 11* (New York, 2001), pp. 93–4.

64 *Ibid.*, p. 116.

65 As noted on the Seven Stories Press website at http://www.sevenstories.com/about/ (accessed 1 July 2005).

66 Arundhati Roy, 'Do Turkeys Enjoy Thanksgiving?', speech at the opening of the Mumbai World Social Forum, 16 January 2004; full text available online at http://www.countercurrents.org/wsf-roy190104.htm (accessed 1 July 2005).

67 Arundhati Roy, 'The Loneliness of Noam Chomsky', *The Hindu*, 24 August 2003.

68 *Ibid*.

69 *Ibid*.

70 Chomsky, *Hegemony or Survival*, p. 7.

71 *Ibid*., p. 14.

72 *Ibid*., p. 62.

73 *Ibid*., p. 143.

74 *Ibid*., p. 156.

75 *Ibid*., p. 185.

76 Keith Windshuttle, 'The Hypocrisy of Noam Chomsky' (2003); full text online at
http://www.newcriterion.com/archive/21/may03/chomsky.htm# (accessed 1 July 2005).

77 Chomsky, *Hegemony or Survival*, p. 235.

78 *Ibid*., pp. 236–7.

4 Reading the Newspapers

1 Harry Kreisler, 'Conversation with Noam Chomsky' (Berkeley, 2002); transcript online at
http://www.chomsky.info/interviews/20020322.htm (accessed 1 July 2005).

2 Noam Chomsky, *Hegemony or Survival* (Crows Nest, NSW, 2003).

3 *Bloomsbury Thematic Dictionary of Quotations* (London, 1988), p. 260.

4 Robert F. Barsky, *Noam Chomsky: A Life of Dissent* (Cambridge, MA, 1998), p. 31.

5 *Ibid*., p. 160.

6 As posted on http://mass-multi-media.com/CRV/ (accessed 1 July 2005).

7 Edward S. Herman and Noam Chomsky, *Manufacturing Consent* (New York, 1988), p. xii.

8 Adam Smith, *Inquiry into the Nature and Causes of the Wealth of Nations* (London, 1776), iv, chapter II.

9 Herman and Chomsky, *Manufacturing Consent*, p. 4.

10 *Ibid.*, p. 13.

11 As posted on the *Washington Post* website at http://www.washington-post.com/wp-srv/onpolitics/watergate/splash.html (accessed 1 July 2005).

12 Herman and Chomsky, *Manufacturing Consent*, p. 27.

13 Cliff Kincaid, 'It Didn't Start or End with Watergate' (AIM, 16 June 2005); full text online at http://www.aim.org/media_monitor/3751_0_2_0_C/ (accessed 2 July 2005).

14 Herman and Chomsky, *Manufacturing Consent*, p. 28.

15 *Ibid.*, p. 287.

16 As posted online at http://en.wikipedia.org/wiki/Manufacturing_Consent:_Noam_Chomsky_and_the_Media (accessed 2 July 2005).

17 Barsky, *Chomsky*, p. 5.

18 As detailed at http://www.imdb.com/name/nm0159008/ (accessed 2 July 2005).

19 The text of Herman's article is available at http://www.zmag.org/content/showarticle.cfm?ItemID=3948 (accessed 2 July 2005).

20 Noam Chomsky, *Necessary Illusions: Thought Control in Democratic Societies* (Boston, 1989), p. 1.

21 *Ibid.*, p. 29.

22 *Ibid.*, p. 3.

23 *Ibid.*, p. 11.

24 *z Magazine* and *z Net* online at http://www.zmag.org/weluser.htm (accessed 2 July 2005).

25 Radio Free Maine's website is at http://www.radiofreemaine.com/RadioFreeMaine.html (accessed 2 July 2005).

26 Noam Chomsky, 'The Journalist from Mars', in *Media Control* (Boston, 2002); text available online at http://www.thirdworldtraveler.com/Chomsky/Journalist_Mars.html (accessed 2 July 2005), unpaginated.

27 *Ibid.*

28 *Ibid.*

Bibliography

For more detailed bibliographies see the 'Official Noam Chomsky Website' at http://www.chomsky.info, which contains much useful material, including excerpts from his activist writings. Select bibliographies of and about Chomsky's work can also be found on-line at http://en.wikipedia.org/wiki/Noam_Chomsky and at http://web.mit.edu/linguistics/www/bibliography/noam.html, the latter being part of Chomsky's MIT home page, but detailing only his works in linguistics. On-line searches will yield many other sites that list Chomsky's work.

By Chomsky

'Review of Skinner', *Language*, 35 (1959)
Aspects of the Theory of Syntax (Cambridge, MA, 1965)
Cartesian Linguistics (New York, 1966)
Language and Mind (New York, 1968)
American Power and the New Mandarins (New York, 1969)
At War with Asia (New York, 1970)
For Reasons of State (London, 1973)
Reflections on Language (New York, 1975)
'Interview', *Leviathan*, 1/1–3 (1977)
Language and Responsibility (New York, 1979)
Morphophonemics of Modern Hebrew (New York, 1979)
Rules and Representations (New York, 1980)
Lectures on Government and Binding: The Pisa Lectures (Dordrecht, 1982)
Knowledge of Language (New York, 1986)
Barriers (Cambridge, MA, 1986)

The Chomsky Reader, ed. James Peck (New York, 1987)

The Managua Lectures (Boston, 1987)

Language and Politics (Montreal, 1988)

'Central America: The Next Phase', posted on *z Magazine* (1988); available
    on-line at http://www.zmag.org/chomsky/articles/z8803-CA-next-
    phase.html (accessed 1 July 2005)

'Scenes from the Uprising' *z Magazine* (1988); text on-line at
    http://www.zmag.org/chomsky/articles/z8807-uprising.html
    (accessed 1 July 2005)

'Interview', *Shmate: A Journal of Progressive Jewish Thought*, 20 (1988)

Necessary Illusions: Thought Control in Democratic Societies (Boston, 1989)

Deterring Democracy (New York, 1991)

The Prosperous Few and the Restless Many (Berkeley, 1993)

Secrets, Lies and Democracy (Berkeley, 1994)

The Minimalist Program (Cambridge, MA, 1995)

Class Warfare: Interviews with David Barsamian (New York, 1996)

Fateful Triangle (Boston, 1999)

Rogue States (Boston, 2000)

New Horizons in the Study of Language and Mind (Cambridge, 2000)

September 11 (New York, 2001)

Media Control (Boston, 2002)

Hegemony or Survival (Australian edn, 2003)

Noam Chomsky: Rebel without a Pause, DVD, 2005

Chomsky On Anarchism (Oakland, 2005)

'Problems and Prospects of the Minimalist Program', course given at LSA,
    25–27 July 2005

with George Miller, 'Finite State Languages', *Information and Control*,
    1 (May 1958), pp. 91–112

with Morris Halle, *The Sound Pattern of English* (New York, 1968)

with Edward S. Herman, *The Washington Connection and Third World Fascism*
    (Boston, 1979)

with Edward S. Herman, *Manufacturing Consent* (New York, 1988)

On Chomsky and Related Topics

Adger, David, *Core Syntax: A Minimalist Approach* (Oxford, 2003)

Austin, John, *How to Do Things with Words* (Oxford, 1961)

Bakunin, Michael, *Bakunin on Anarchy*, ed. and trans. Sam Dolgoff (New York, 1972)

Barsky, Robert, F., *Noam Chomsky: A Life of Dissent* (Cambridge, 1997)

Bloomfield, Leonard, *Language* (New York, 1933)

Bloomsbury Thematic Dictionary Of Quotations (London, 1988)

Burns, Alex, 'Operation Mindcrime: The Selling of Noam Chomsky', 2001; text on-line at http://www.disinfo.com/archive/pages/article/id589/pg1/ (accessed 1 July 2005)

Chepesiuk, Ron, *Sixties Radicals, Then and Now* (Jefferson, NC, 1995)

Chomsky, Carol, *The Acquisition of Syntax in Children From Five to Ten* (Cambridge, MA, 1969)

Crystal, David, *A Dictionary of Linguistics and Phonetics* (Oxford, 1991)

Davidson, Donald and Jaako Hintikka, eds, *Words and Objections: Essays on the Work of W. V. Quine* (Dordrecht, 1969)

Dougherty, Ray C., *Natural Language Computing* (Hillsdale, NJ, 1994)

Feinberg, Harriet, *Elsie Chomsky: A Life in Jewish Education* (Cambridge, MA, 1999)

Guérin, Daniel, *Anarchism: From Theory to Practice*, trans. Mary Klopper (New York, 1970)

Guy, Camille, 'The Truth is Out There', *Listener* (22 May 2004)

Harman, Gilbert, ed., *On Noam Chomsky: Critical Essays* (New York, 1974)

Harris, Zellig S., *Methods in Structural Linguistics* (Chicago, 1951)

Harris, Randy Allen, *The Linguistics Wars* (New York, 1993)

Hoffer, Eric, *The True Believer: Thoughts on the Nature of Mass Movements* (New York, 1958)

Hughes, Samuel, 'The Way They Were (and Are)', *University of Pennsylvania Gazette* (2001)

Jakobson, Roman, *Selected Writings 1: Phonological Studies* (The Hague, 1962)

Kayne, Richard, *The Antisymmetry of Syntax* (Cambridge, MA, 1994)

Kedward, Roderick, *The Anarchists* (London, 1971)

Kincaid, Cliff, 'It Didn't Start or End With Watergate' *AIM*, 16 June 2005; full text at http://www.aim.org/media_monitor/3751_0_2_0_C/ (accessed 2 July 2005)

Kreisler, Harry, 'Conversation with Noam Chomsky', Berkeley, 2002; transcript available on http://www.chomsky.info/interviews/20020322.htm (accessed 1 July 2005)

Lees, Robert, *The Grammar of English Nominalisations* (The Hague, 1960)

Lévi-Strauss, Claude, *Tristes Tropiques* (New York, 1963)

Lipstadt, Deborah E, 'Deniers, Relativists and Pseudo-Scholarship', *Dimensions*, 6/1 (1991)

Lyons, John, *Chomsky* (London, 1991)

Mailer, Norman, *Armies of the Night* (New York, 1968)

Marx, Karl, *The Civil War in France* (1871; New York, 1941)

Matthews, G. H., *Hidatsa Syntax* (The Hague, 1965)

Matthews, P. H., *Grammatical Theory in the United States from Bloomfield to Chomsky* (Cambridge, 1993)

McGilvray, James, *Chomsky* (Cambridge, 1999)

Mechelli Andrea, et al., 'Neurolinguistics: Structural Plasticity in the Bilingual Brain', *Nature*, 431 (2004), p. 757

Mitford, Jessica, *The Trial of Dr. Spock, the Rev. William Sloane Coffin, Jr., Michael Ferber, Mitchell Goodman, and Marcus Raskin* (New York, 1969)

Otero, Carlos, ed., *Noam Chomsky: Critical Assessments* (London, 1994)

Rai, Milan, *Chomsky's Politics* (New York, 1995)

Ramaiah, L. S. and T. V. Prafulla Chandra, *Noam Chomsky: A Bibliography* (Gurgaon, 1984)

Rizzi, Luigi, *The Structure of CP and IP – The Cartography of Syntactic Structures* (Oxford, 2004)

Rocker, Rudolph, *Anarcho-Syndicalism – Theory and Practice: An Introduction to a Subject Which the Spanish War Has Brought into Overwhelming Prominence* (London, 1938)

——, *Anarchosyndicalism* (London, 1938)

——, *Anarchism and Anarcho-Syndicalism* (London, 1973)

——, 'Anarchism and Sovietism', text available on http://flag.blackened.net/rocker/soviet.htm (accessed 1 July 2005)

Roy, Arundhati, 'The Loneliness Of Noam Chomsky', *The Hindu* (24 August 2003)

——, 'Do Turkeys Enjoy Thanksgiving?', speech at the Opening of the Mumbai World Social Forum, 16 January 2004; full text available on-line at http://www.countercurrents.org/wsf-roy190104.htm (accessed 1 July 2005)

Russell, Bertrand, *History of Western Philosophy* (London, 1946)
——, *Roads to Freedom* (3rd edn, London, 1948)
Santillan, Diego Abad de, *After the Revolution* (New York, 1937)
Saussure, Ferdinand de, *Course in General Linguistics* (New York, 1959)
Skinner, B. F., *Verbal Behavior* (New York, 1957)
Smith, Adam, *The Wealth of Nations* (London, 1776)
Smith, Neil, *Chomsky, Ideas and Ideals* (Cambridge, 1999)
Trubetzkoy, N., *Principles of Phonology* (Berkeley, 1939)
Volkery, Carsten, 'Noam Chomsky, Der Grossvater der Amerika-Kritiker',
    Spiegel Online, 25 March 2005; text available on-line at
    http://www.spiegel.de/politik/deutschland/0,1518,348276,00.html
    (accessed 3 July 2005)
Windshuttle, Keith, 'The Hypocrisy of Noam Chomsky', 2003; full text
    available on-line at http://www.newcriterion.com/archive/21/may03/
    chomsky.htm# (accessed 1 July 2005)
Zinn, Howard, 'Against Discouragement', speech delivered at Spelman
    College, 15 May 2005; transcript of speech on-line at
    http://www.zmag.org/content/showarticle.cfm?SectionID=41&ItemID
    =7934 (accessed 2 July 2005)

Acknowledgements

Many thanks to Carol and Noam Chomsky, who have generously assisted me in this project. Thanks to Steven Roger Fischer for having recommended me. Thanks to family, friends and colleagues who read drafts, made valuable comments and otherwise provided encouragement to keep me going. Any shortcomings are mine alone.

Photo Acknowledgements

The author and publishers wish to express their thanks to the below sources of illustrative material and/or permission to reproduce it:

Photos courtesy of Carol Chomsky: pp. 6, 8, 11, 17, 19, 20, 21, 22, 43, 52, 113, 119, 138; photo courtesy of Steven Roger Fischer: p. 125; photo courtesy of Rosamond Halle: p. 34; photo Sumire Kunieda: p. 123; cover photo courtesy of Pantheon Books, New York: p. 127; photo courtesy of the George Orwell Archive, University College London: p. 72; photo courtesy of the Bertrand Russell Archive, McMaster University, Hamilton, Ontario, Canada: p. 73; photo Marion S. Trikosko/Library of Congress, Washington, DC (US News & World Report Magazine Photograph Collection; LC-USZ62-134155): p. 79; photo Torrini Fotogiornalismo: p. 24; image courtesy of Jeffrey Weston, Postmodernhaircut.com: p. 60.